THE CHILDHOOD CONCLUSIONS FIX

Turning Negative Self-Talk Around

Other books by the same author

Alight

The Eldest Daughter Effect
(with Wies Enthoven)

THE CHILDHOOD CONCLUSIONS FIX

Turning Negative Self-Talk Around

LISETTE SCHUITEMAKER

FINDHORN PRESS

Published in 2017 by Findhorn Press, Scotland

ISBN 978-1-84409-734-0

Edited by Jacqui Lewis
Cover photo by Odan Jaeger
Author photos by Albert Schuitemaker (child); Hans Hiltermann (adult)
Cover design by Richard Crookes
Interior design and illustration by Damian Keenan
Printed and bound in the EU

DISCLAIMER

The information in this book is given in good faith and is neither
intended to diagnose any physical or mental condition nor to serve
as a substitute for informed medical advice or care.
Please contact your health professional for medical advice and
treatment. Neither author nor publisher can be held liable by any
person for any loss or damage whatsoever which may arise from the
use of this book or any of the information therein.

Published by
Findhorn Press
117-121 High Street,
Forres IV36 1AB,
Scotland, UK

t +44 (0)1309 690582
f +44 (0)131 777 2711
e info@findhornpress.com
www.findhornpress.com

Contents

Introduction

Our childhood conclusions mirror our greatest gifts. Where we feel the most insecure is where we hide our truest treasures.

We all come into this world bearing gifts. Within us as tiny babies lie innate abilities to open our hearts and connect to others, to make people come alive through our mere presence. As divine creations of consciousness in formation we harbour the gifts to feel and excite joy, to laugh and be funny, to experience deep concern and empathy, to be inspired as well as inspiring. We are born with the capacity to feel exuberance, to act autonomously, to relish reverence and gratitude and, most of all, to show and share love.

In the end, our connection with others and advancing their well-being is what makes a good life. Growing up to get to that point of contributing in our very own way, however, bears liking to the game of hide and seek. Through painful experiences we resolve to hide part of our inner riches, as bringing them out in the open feels too risky. We'll be damaged and hurt or even ridiculed and banished if we show our true colours. At least, that is what we come to believe on the basis of experiences in our young years. Yet, our innate urge to meet our life's purpose has us seek exactly what we're trying to hide so we may bring out our gifts and fulfil the promise of our lives.

A word on self-talk

Do we dare to fully incarnate, assume that we are enough, live our own life, put our trust in others and embrace our quirkiness? We may be inclined to shrug our shoulders as if this is not a big deal. Our life, however, is one big string of choices made moment to moment. These choices are the object of the inner conversations that we are conducting with ourselves.

There is no person in the world we talk to as much as we talk to ourselves. We may be lecturers or teachers or work behind a counter or a cash register that has people on the other side all day; our profession may be waiting tables, tending bars or being talk-show hosts, we may discuss every little detail of our lives with our partner or garrulous girlfriends – but still, the extent of our talking to others pales compared to how much we talk to ourselves.

Once we start to pay attention to our ongoing inner conversations, we will soon notice that we are not speaking with one voice only. A wide variety of characters take it in turns to claim centre stage when they are triggered to come to the fore. We may notice that we whine inwardly like a small child who feels not at all up to the demands of life. Moments later, we can find ourselves in a different mood as another inner voice starts to rant and rave that we need to be in control of our destiny, of other people, of life itself. Another inner part of ourselves may be given to bitter berating of ourselves for not behaving well, having said the wrong thing – again! We are on repeat most of the time, telling ourselves the same stories over and over again, getting into the same inner arguments, blaming the same people, cautioning ourselves to hold together, hold on, hold in, hold up or hold back.

The trouble is that we tend to believe what we think. Our most adamant inner voices shrink our awareness until we think what they tell us is true. Yet, we are not our inner voices, we just have them. Thoughts are just thoughts and there is no need to believe everything we think. Especially not when our thoughts arise from the perspective of the small child we once were who felt they didn't belong or weren't good enough. As a child we may have felt we had no power over our life or that we needed to keep life under control and fit in at all times. Even if we have entertained such a thought a thousand times, that doesn't mean it's true. There is no need to believe everything we think.

A handful of conclusions

I've always found it odd that in school we learn the grammar of our language, the history of our part of the world and the logic of mathematics, but not the grammar, history and logic of ourselves. I feel strongly that we ought to be taught basic models of psychology as we grow up.

Wilhelm Reich was one of the first psychiatrists, at the beginning of the 20th century. He discovered that, as different as we may look in our outward appearance, the kinds of thoughts we think about ourselves are not that different at all. I first came across his theory of the character defence structures when I studied at the Brennan School of Healing. Like my fellow students, I was astonished by the small number of distinct categories of thoughts that we usually entertain. Only a handful!

"Why didn't I learn this insightful model before?" and "Why aren't we all aware of the conclusions we jump to in our early youth?" Those two questions impelled me to write this book. I wanted a kinder term than the forbidding "character defence structures" coined by Reich's students. Instead I named the five sources of our ongoing inner dialogues our "childhood conclusions".

None of us will have all the characteristics and mannerisms of a childhood conclusion as I describe them, nor will the self-talk from each of the conclusions be as neatly separated in us as on the pages of a book. It is, however, helpful to be able to categorize the various streams in our ongoing inner conversations. Once we can identify the thoughts coming out of each of the five childhood conclusions, we will be able to see how they reinforce one another. During the course of our childhood years, we have inevitably jumped to more than one conclusion.

Our most negative self-talk hides our most precious gifts. We can turn our restrictive self-talk around so we can shine in the gifts that lie on the other side of it. As if that is not reward enough, insight into our basic childhood conclusions provides better understanding of our own reactions as well as those of others. Through the model of the childhood conclusions we will be able to respond with more clemency to the previously incomprehensible way colleagues behave, as we realize what causes them to react the way they do. As parents, we will become aware of the unavoidable conclusions of our offspring. There is no escape – they will draw childhood conclusions, just as we did when we were small, and our parents before us.

In this book, I describe the gifts hidden by the five childhood conclusions we jump to when we are small, as a result of inevitable unfortunate interactions with our parents or other adults close to us. Drawing on my own life and my professional experience as well as on contemporary books, movies, talks and interviews, I describe how it is to grow up with each conclusion as well as what they bring us. A positive present begins with comprehension of the distinct elements of our negative self-talk and the childhood conclusions they arise from. On that basis we can turn around self-deprecating thoughts, heal those early wounds and allow our gifts to burgeon.

A brief sketch

Let's begin with a brief sketch of the five childhood conclusions in the order in which they are usually drawn at the ages of a newborn, a baby, a toddler and a young child. A word of caution before reading: when I first read my innermost thoughts written down in one of the books of Dr Barbara Brennan, I was shocked. Sitting in a cafe in New York where we lived for a semester, I looked around surreptitiously. Other people were having tea, chatting, unaware of me feeling utterly vulnerable now that my deep-seated conviction that I would never be good enough turned out to be a thought the majority of us nurse. I felt horribly found out when my observation that I didn't seem to feel as much as other people was described as the usual presenting complaint of people who had felt they didn't fit in with their family. I remember gaping at proving much more predictable and "normal" than I had taken myself to be. Don't we all want to feel like one of a kind? A whirlwind of feeling offended brought the impulse to throw the book into a corner and not go to this famed healing school at all.

I didn't act on that impulse, fortunately. To this day I am grateful that I put myself through that school with its four years of immersion into the childhood conclusions we all jump to. I was ready to let go of who I was in order to become who I am. So, be forewarned. Reading these short summaries of the childhood conclusions may bring the relief of recognition as well as a jolt – and may start you on a joyful journey of discovery.

1 CHILDHOOD CONCLUSION
"I'm not welcome, I must go elsewhere."

NEGATIVE SELF-TALK

"If only I were somewhere else, in another place, another time – maybe then I'd belong and feel welcome and safe. I find the world harsh, hard and unpleasant. I don't know if I really want to be here. I take refuge in the world of dreams, in higher spheres where it's quiet, beautiful and harmonious. The contact with those domains keeps me alive."

The first childhood conclusion arises from the existential terror of the newborn. Are we even welcome on this planet? Maybe our mother lacked confidence, unsure if she really wanted the baby or if she could cope. An infant may be alarmed by a door slamming, a voice shouting. In fright, our small body tenses up. The first neural pathways being laid down in the brain record these initial, adversarial physical reactions.

People with this childhood conclusion are often highly original and gifted. We have maintained our natural connection with the realms of spirit that we hail from and may have a hard time being down to earth. With our heads in the clouds, we may find it difficult to keep our lives together. More often than we'd like, we feel we don't truly belong – which is a false notion as we are here, so of course we belong.

2 CHILDHOOD CONCLUSION

"There isn't enough, I am not enough."

NEGATIVE SELF-TALK

"I'm not good, smart, fit and savvy enough. I never get back as much as I give, but I don't want to ask people for anything. I will only be disappointed. Again. I have to be able to do everything for myself. If only I had more time, money, capacity – there is never enough."

The mainspring of the second childhood conclusion is fear of deficiency. A small baby suffers agonies if someone doesn't show up to feed it when it has woken up hungry, or when it is returned to the crib before it feels wholly satisfied. The little body craves more food, more time being held and cuddled and touched. The impression arises that there isn't enough: not enough food, not enough time, not enough attention for me: I am not enough.

These babies grow into adults who are forever plagued by thoughts that we don't have enough time, have not read enough, are not funny, skinny or accomplished enough. We become adored performers, actors, anchors. People with this childhood conclusion are endlessly curious scientists and journalists with the gift of the gab. Seeking to stand out in some way, we succeed in getting the attention we long for. Trouble is, it's never enough, because that insatiable hunger for more will return – until we realize we have always been and will always be enough.

3 CHILDHOOD CONCLUSION

"What do I know – have it your way."

NEGATIVE SELF-TALK

"I'll just go along with the others, that'll be the easiest. I don't really know what I want, so I'd rather let the others choose. That way I won't make any enemies. It does make me feel powerless, though. As if I'm a nobody. I tend to play the innocent – I can't help it, and it's safer, if you know what I mean. But then, I end up feeling stupid, and that sucks too. So, I'm stuck, I guess."

Underlying the third childhood conclusion are feelings of confusion and impotence. Toddlers like to keep their parents and other grown-ups happy but in our innocence, we do things that make them angry. Some of us as young children had things happen to us that we didn't want but were powerless to prevent. We are furious that our boundaries were not respected by someone we knew, but, afraid to jeopardize the love of our parents, we kept quiet. We swallowed our frustration and fury, resigned ourselves to our fate and consoled ourselves by eating and cracking jokes at our own expense.

Beyond our apparent lethargy lies a well of creativity. Feeling like a victim ourselves, we have developed huge empathy and behind our happy face lies deep compassion for the plight of others. The false image this childhood conclusion paints is that we have no power over our lives, and so we tend to give up even before we've begun. In truth, all of us are ultimately the directors of our own lives. We are free to live our own destiny. Becoming aware of that freedom is an inner job that begins with the question "What if my body, my creativity and my life were truly mine?"

CHILDHOOD CONCLUSION

"I must be in control."

NEGATIVE SELF-TALK

"In the end no one is fully trustworthy. I love people and I have many friends but I also keep an eye on everybody, so I know exactly where they're at. Never again will I be betrayed by someone I trusted as I make a point of always knowing what comes next. I like being ahead of the game as it gives me a sense of control."

In childhood games we assume grandiose roles. We can easily imagine ourselves as princes and heroines, saving the world and everyone in it, or as the true partner of Mummy or Daddy, whom we will later, of course, marry. We take a caress or a look as proof of this bond and then feel betrayed when the parent turns out not to see us as their life partner. Our hearts break for the first time: our naive trust is dented and this is so painful that we resolve never to let that happen again.

Cultivating our sensitivity to other people's motives, we become superb strategists, people who look ahead and like to keep things under control. No matter how commanding we are, however, life takes unexpected turns and control remains elusive, which creates stress and tension even though we continue to look self-assured.

We have big hearts that can easily fit our whole family, wide circle of friends and worthy causes to fight for. Our strategic insight and our charisma make people achieve more than they thought themselves capable of, and have a great time too. We are well-loved and if we could find it in ourselves to begin to trust life, we could do even much more good than we are already doing.

5 CHILDHOOD CONCLUSION

"I must conform to fit in."

NEGATIVE SELF-TALK

"What should I wear to show the world I know the codes? Others think I am competent, but I am afraid to be found out as a fake. I have learned to get on well with people in all situations, yet I can't help but keep a distance. Outwardly, my life looks perfect. Inside I feel empty and cold. I just don't feel as much as other people. Is this all there is to life? I'd better keep up the false facade so at least people think I'm capable."

For some of us, the way our parents shaped their lives doesn't resonate, and as the odd one out we conclude we must be a bit off. It may come to pass that we have wanted to show our parents how much we loved them, but that at an age of budding sexuality we did so in a way that created embarrassment.

As a child, we sensed we had overstepped a boundary without ever having known it was there. We take fright as we think we might do so again, and so decide instead to follow suit and produce only desired ways of behaving. We fret endlessly over our appearance, what to wear and what to say, and scrutinize our behaviours long after anyone continues to remember what we said or did. We become keen observers of others and, as chameleons, put in any situation we can "do as the Romans do".

The challenge is to give up trying to be perfect as that is unattainable anyway, to thaw and get in touch again with our emotions and our very own quirkiness. A positive present begins with our rediscovery of our authentic selves. We can be who we are, quirks and all. Life is quirky anyway.

Taking the test

If you want to find out which childhood conclusions you have predominantly drawn, do the test on my website *lisetteschuitemaker.com*. Going through the 25 questions quickly, clicking the button at the bottom and getting the results will give you an impression of the measure in which each of the childhood conclusions operate in your life.

Turning our childhood thoughts

Turning a childhood conclusion is my term for transforming the unhelpful thoughts that stem from early life experiences and interpretations by allowing the underlying emotions to flow and dissolve. A first step towards tending the garden of our minds is to begin to recognize the thoughts produced by our childhood conclusions.

These three clues are helpful in identifying thoughts that stem from big conclusions that we drew when we were only very small:

1. The same thoughts keep coming back

We may all be familiar with thoughts that go around and around in our heads without getting us anywhere. Maybe we find ourselves repeating the same argument to justify an action, blame someone else or commiserate on our situation like we did a thousand times before. These kinds of endlessly recurring thoughts that get us worked up or bogged down arise from our childhood conclusions.

2. These thoughts stress us out

Something *must* happen and it must happen *now!* Someone *must* be told the truth this very moment or… This is no ordinary "must". This is a must with a charge that is a clear signal that a childhood conclusion has been triggered. We *must* know what happens next, we *must* get people to listen to us, we *must* keep in line, we *must* buy those trendy jeans or we *must* put up with what others want. These kinds of thoughts are like a merry-go-round that keeps spinning without giving us a chance to hop off. Faster and faster we go, while staying forever in the same place.

3. These thoughts often contain the words "always" or "never"

A third characteristic of self-limiting thoughts generated by our childhood conclusions is that they tend to contain the words "always" or "never". When we are small, our family is the world to us and if we feel somehow wrong or lacking in their eyes, we think everyone will always disapprove of us and we will never find our place in this world.

It may take some practice to identify recurring thoughts. What makes it hard is that we are in the habit of going along with our thoughts instead of watching them shapeshifting by like clouds in the sky. Once we are on to them, we can greet recurring thoughts like old friends: "Ah, there you are again."

Neuropsychiatrist Dr Daniel Siegel has written extensively on the ability to understand where our thoughts come from, to know our mind and direct our thoughts and feelings rather than be driven by them. "Mindsight" is the term he coined for this aptitude. In his best-selling book by the same title, he compares the dexterity to focus our attention on our inner world to picking up a scalpel in order to resculpt our brain. "Through the cultivation of the skill of mindsight," he states, "we can resculpt our neural pathways and stimulate the growth of areas of the brain that are crucial to mental health and well-being." But change never just happens, he warns. It's something we have to work at.

His view is substantiated by the work of cell biologist Bruce Lipton, PhD, author of *The Biology of Belief*. He first had the insight 30 years ago that he could change his life by changing his beliefs. He was instantly energized, he writes, because he realized that there was a science-based path that would take him from his job as a perennial "victim" to his new job as "co-creator" of his destiny. "Especially in the last decade," he says now, "the belief that we are frail, biochemical machines controlled by genes is giving way to an understanding that we are powerful creators of our lives and the world in which we live."

Turn our thoughts, change our lives

Changing our beliefs to change our lives – that is the idea behind turning the loops of thought that our childhood conclusions keep whispering to us long after we have grown into adults. "Name it to tame it" is number two of the 12 whole-brain strategies that Dr Daniel Siegel and parenting expert Tina Payne Bryson describe in *The Whole-Brain Child*. The phrase is the authors' shorthand for the strategy of allowing a child who is upset to tell their story. Taking the time for them to relay what happened in detail reassures the child that the adult cares. Retelling the story will also serve to calm the child down. "In fact, research shows that merely assigning a name or label to what we feel literally calms down the activity of the emotional circuitry in the right hemisphere," the authors say.

Being willing to give the child we once were the time to recount their story, relive the emotions and thus let go is exactly what the five steps of turning the childhood conclusion propose. The first of the five steps is to begin to recognize the recurring patterns that bring us back into child consciousness. Some thoughtful watching will soon reveal which of the childhood conclusions they stem from.

Since we ourselves are now the adult who will work with our own inner childhood memories and conclusions, the second step is to focus on who we have become. Through all the trials and tribulations of our life we have grown into who we are today. We ground ourselves firmly in the present, in our strengths and capacities, in the life we have built for ourselves.

Thirdly we thank the childhood part of us that has stepped up in an effort to protect us from further fear, lack, shame, pain or embarrassment. In essence, we thank ourselves for how we have tried to avoid suffering. Receiving heartfelt gratitude, even from ourselves, relaxes our whole system. Then we are ready to be a container for old emotions we are consciously going to evoke with the aim of letting them go.

The fourth step is to revisit the fear, panic or pain we felt as a child while being centred in the adult we have become. It's as if we sit down with a child to hear what has happened. We can deal with their anguish, their pain and their struggle. We can let them feel they are safe with us. We all naturally know how to do that. Now we can practise extending the same loving attention to ourselves as we consciously evoke feelings we have been trying to avoid and repress since childhood. When they come up, they will gather momentum – but we are adults. We can weather a storm. We know that, even if it seems to be lasting an eternity, it will pass. Then we come out the other end, released, relieved and with more capacity to express our essence – which is what step five is about.

A healing response

Each of the following chapters also contains a description of a healing response that is useful to apply when you want to stand strong but negative self-talk arises. A healing response may sound airy-fairy, but fact is that we influence each other's energy all the time. Who doesn't feel uplifted when a friend greets us effusively out of obvious joy to see us again? Who hasn't gone to a movie feeling dead beat only to come out fully re-energized by its happy ending? Who has not had the experience of having someone cry on your shoulder and you just sat with them without saying much until they upped and left, saying how much better you had made them feel?

A healing response works something like that. Through consciously regulating our interior state of being we can relax and uplift ourselves and others in no time. As we infuse our cells with a sense of well-being, this will communicate to the cells of someone standing or sitting across from us, or even someone who is some distance away but whom we hold in our awareness.

Siegel and Payne Bryson explain this phenomenon of each of us being able to influence others emotionally through the discovery of mirror neurons in the early 1990s. In Italy, a group of neuroscientists had implanted electrodes in a macaque monkey to monitor individual neurons. A certain neuron in the monkey's brain fired when it ate a peanut. When one of the scientists ate a peanut in view of the monkey, to their surprise the very same neuron fired in the monkey's brain. This is how the researchers discovered that the monkey's brain was activated merely by watching the action of another. The research on how mirror neurons work in humans is still ongoing, but findings indicate that we can mirror not only actions but emotions as well. This is why a feel-good movie warms our heart and cheers us up.

This is also why we can make others feel good by choosing to activate positive emotions in ourselves, to smile as we walk the street, to radiate loving kindness.

Healing responses are tailored to each of the childhood conclusions and the kind of thoughts they produce. To deal with the conclusion that we are not welcome and must go elsewhere, we fill ourselves with a sense of being welcome. Hit by thoughts of not having or being enough, we can respond by fostering a sense of general enoughness; not too little, not too much but exactly enough. Overwhelmed, confused, terrified of showing what we've got, we can kindle the flame of freedom in our bellies. When we feel the urge to keep control, we go to our heart and let love spread through our whole system. In the grip of thoughts that tell us we need to project a perfect image or be excommunicated, we invite our sense of authenticity to grow, knowing it is real.

Practising these responses on ourselves will help us relax each time a thought from a childhood conclusion tries to force us into a narrowed awareness of what is happening. As with the oxygen masks on a plane, the person to give aid to first is ourselves. Once we are back in balance, we may want to extend the sense of wholeness to others.

Travelling recently I sat next to a fidgety man. To be honest, my first reaction was apprehension, but fortunately I soon remembered that a different response could benefit both of us. Realizing that he might feel nervous to be leaving the control of his fate in the hands of the pilot, I inwardly nurtured a sense of infinite trust. This helped me shift from irritation to open-heartedness and after a minute or so he picked up his book and started to read with happy concentration. That's the point with the healing response – to remember it.

1

Welcoming our existence

CHILDHOOD CONCLUSION

"I am not welcome, I must go elsewhere."

NEGATIVE SELF-TALK

"A mistake has been made. I am not welcome. I can't be with these people who are too coarse, too crude for me. I need eternal beauty, peace and quiet. I don't belong here. I must go elsewhere."

CORE GIFTS

aesthetics, sensitivity, spirituality, vision

Within the immeasurable vastness of the universe, tucked in a corner of a small solar system, here we are on our beautiful blue Planet Earth. Whether from a spiritual or a physics point of view, the realization that our earthly life is part of a much bigger context immediately broadens our vision. This larger framing of an evolving cosmic life expressed in myriads of entities, us as humans among them, gives meaning and purpose to life. Some people will reject the spiritual interpretation, but many of us do not need reminding of the heavens as that is where our attention usually soars. We may, in fact, find it hard and even hazardous to come down to earth. This is illustrated by the predicament of a highly successful Dutch entrepreneur by the name of Jim.

After selling his latest business venture he was quite a disconsolate millionaire. "I have had a glowing career, I've turned difficult companies around, sold them and earned more money than I will ever be able to spend, but if you care to know the truth," he said to me, "I have yet to set foot on this earth." Financially he could do as he liked, but, no longer having work to distract

21

him, he initially found it hard to bring structure into his days. He lounged about and found no fulfilment in a life of pleasure. He read the news for hours on end, only to end up exasperated by the brutality with which humans make a mess for one another. People, of course, expected him to be over the moon about his good fortune. "That's exactly the issue," Jim said with a sorry smile. "Over the moon is precisely where I hang out. Way beyond in outer space. I am not here with my attention at all, but I think the time has come to make this spacecraft land."

He had been feeling antsy for longer than he cared to remember. "I've lived in several countries but I have never really felt like I belonged. I've never felt at home anywhere, not even in my own body. Or in my own life," is how he described his flighty condition. As well as disconsolate, he was rather angry; it seemed as if everything irked and irritated him. Could it be that he was troubled by the imperfection of existence? "Yeah," he said, with a grin but without his eyes joining in the mirth, "I could put it like that. And I want rid of it. ET come home."

Half of us

Many of us suffer from the uncanny feeling of not quite being welcome here on earth, as if a mistake had been made and we should not have ended up in a body in the first place. We yearn for the peaceful perfection that we sense in the heavens, the oneness that was our habitat before being born. If we are not beset by these kinds of feelings ourselves, we all know people who live among the stars rather than on this crude earth plane. Theory has it that at least half of us are escapists who prefer to move up, up and away. We tend to be half here, half there, out and about in the vast realms of imagination, dreams and fantasy, the spheres of spirit.

Under pressure, but often for no easily identifiable reason, we become restless. Agitation washes over us like an incoming tide. Our thoughts become jumpy and have us believe we are not where we ought to be. We had better get a move on fast. Out of the confinement of this room, this job, this relationship or this town. On to the next scene that might, just might be where we can finally rest our buzzing head. Away from the relentless bombardment of daily impulses that are way too loud and too many to process. Away also from the intensity of the emotions of others that, in this sensitive state of not being fully in our bodies, we pick up from everyone we are in touch with, and sometimes even from people just passing by. The jitters tell us anywhere is better than here; but once we've arrived somewhere else our agitated self-talk will tell us this isn't the right spot either. In this mercurial way, as long as we listen to our skittish impulses of needing to flee, our thoughts will keep us moving as the perfect peace we seek remains out of sight.

Our first childhood conclusion

Jim's story of believing for so long that he did not belong here on earth is a textbook example of how as newborns we translate our first sensory experiences into a childhood conclusion. Later, when we have words, this childhood conclusion will tell us over and over "I'm not welcome, I don't belong here, I must go elsewhere."

Jim was born prematurely and in anguish over her firstborn his mother did not dare bond with the little bag of bones that he was. Terrified that he would not make it, she shied away from him in a desperate effort to protect herself from the unspeakable pain of the loss she was afraid she was going to suffer. Imagine how that must be for a tiny newborn. Just out of the warm protection of the womb a baby's body instinctively craves touch, warmth, loving contact. Along with physical care and nurture, the helpless infant needs to be held, cuddled and cherished in order to grow. It needs the sensation of warmth, skin to skin, of drowsy fullness in the belly, of its miniature muscles flexing in response to a loving touch. It needs to be comforted and nurtured to so it can start to feel safe in this world where the light is so bright and the noise so loud compared to the padded place where it has just spent nine months, growing from two cells into a fully developed mini human being.

Like Jim, many of us go through a sensory experience very early in our lives that makes us feel unsafe and uncared for, somehow not welcome. From a warm womb, we fell on to a cold steel table, we were slapped into taking our first breath, we no longer felt the contact with our mother, we were exhausted by the long struggle through the birth canal, perhaps we went straight into an incubator. Immediately upon our birth, sensory images began streaming into our rapidly connecting brain cells. Many of us are born out of the ardent desire of our parents to have children. Even then, the complex processes of pregnancy and birth can at some point convey an impression of us not being welcome. At the very origins of our self-imagery the hunch that something has gone terribly wrong, and that we should not really have been born, is pervasive.

Fathers and mothers in other circumstances might not have wanted a child. Others may be terrified that they won't be able to cope with the responsibility a needy little one brings. Some of us were born to mothers who had been abused or raped, or to parents who felt too young, unstable or unhappy to have a child. If a mother is fearful of being pregnant, the first cluster of cells that attaches itself to the wall of the womb might contract, from an apprehended hostility. This very early first subtle contraction will turn into an inherent response in our body that, once we are born, we will inexplicably feel a lot of the time. In essence, the rejection had nothing to do with us. It was an involuntary result of the anxiety of a mother who, for reasons her own, was scared of this pregnancy.

Some traditions explain a strong sense of not being welcome through reincarnation and our experiences in previous lives. We are inclined to take all of the above personally and interpret our nervy nature as a result of being born in an adverse world. This feeling of having been unwelcome may be reinforced by parents who are preoccupied with their own lives, are in a relationship that is breaking up or are going through a difficult time financially. We may pick up on a general sense of unsafety by being born during a war or a famine, or any form of societal upheaval that causes stress in the family.

Whatever the circumstances, the parents are not to blame. All parents do the best they can at any given time. Neither are we to blame for how we were born or how we began the process of incarnation, and of growing our bodies as best we could through eating and sleeping. We each have our story, but it is the present that offers us the choice of how to view our past and move beyond it so we can live our essential gifts.

No difficult babies

Jim's mother didn't dare to bond with her baby because she was afraid of the immense grief she would suffer if she were to lose her premature firstborn. She kept to herself as no one was really there for her in the stern, Dutch Protestant countryside village where Jim grew up.

Usually parents who cannot give love to their babies are in dire need of loving attention themselves. Mothers who suffer from post-natal depression also struggle to open their hearts to their newborn. They surely need loving care themselves, as they disappear into darkness just at the time they might have imagined being full of the bliss and joy of motherhood. Loving care and understanding is needed, too, by parents who feel anger, despair and guilt as they feel like the unlucky ones to whom fate has dealt a difficult baby.

Psychoanalytic psychotherapist Sue Gerhardt doesn't believe in difficult babies. Parents, in her view, are needed as a sort of emotional coach who helps the baby regulate its feelings by identifying with their needs as well as through responding non-verbally. The gist of her book *Why Love Matters* is explained in its subtitle *How affection shapes a baby's brain*. "The difficult thing about babies is that they need care almost continuously for many months," she writes. "Each baby has a unique personal store of genes which can be activated by experience." She attributes the outcome of the dynamic interaction between baby and parents to the latter. She cites researchers who have failed to identify any such thing as a "difficult" baby in the early weeks of life, suggesting this is largely the perception of the parents. Then she makes the wonderful observation that there may in fact, from the point of view of the baby, be "difficult" parents. These parents tend to fall into two types: neglectful or intrusive.

"At the the neglectful end of the scale," she writes, "there are depressed mothers who find it very hard to respond to their babies, who tend to be apathetic and withdrawn and don't make eye contact with their babies or pick them up much except to clean them or feed them." At the intrusive end of the scale, she portrays the mother who might also be depressed but who is much more angry, even if only covertly. "This is a more expressive kind of mother who at some level resents the baby's demands and feels hostile to him. She may convey this to the baby by picking him up abruptly and holding him stiffly." Although in this passage she mentions only mothers, she concludes by observing, "Fortunately most parents instinctively provide enough attention and sensitivity to their babies to ensure their emotional security. But what seems to be most crucial for the baby is the extent to which the parent or caregiver is emotionally available and present for him, to notice his signals and regulate his states; something which the baby cannot yet do for himself except in the most rudimentary ways, like sucking his own fingers when hungry or turning his head away from distressing stimulation."

Infants, of course, are unaware of the predicaments of their parents, their fears and uncertainties. For a newborn, the first impressions of the world outside of the womb are crucial. When as babies we experience hostility, in whatever form, in the first hours or days of our lives, we implicate ourselves as to us everything and everyone is still one big blob of beingness. Over time we will come out of the merger with our mother and develop the capacity to distinguish between ourselves and everything else; but in this primitive phase of sensory perception, that level of development is still far over the horizon. In these early days frightening occurrences like loud noises or harsh treatment make our little body feel unsafe. Instinctually we form the impression that we are not welcome, that we do not belong, that we should not be here at all. These first impressions go on to play a huge part in how many of us come to look at life.

Not all of us draw this first childhood conclusion that will have us on the run for a lot of the time. A disconnection with the mother may be the blueprint for the identity of one baby and not have an effect on another. While the nature vs nurture debate is still on, my take on this is that the nature of our particular innate gifts is a determining factor in how we interpret what happens in the way of nurture in our early life. This first childhood conclusion is often drawn by those who come into this life with a sensitive nature, with a predisposition towards the arts and with an intrinsic openness to spirituality.

Head space

Many would have looked puzzled, but thirty-something Taylor knows exactly what is meant by the question of whether she ever goes down to her legs or if they are like a cellar that she never enters. "Nobody has ever asked me this," she says, rather astonished, "but it's true. I only live in my head, and it's extremely busy up there. All my thoughts are in a jumble and everything seems equally important. Usually, it takes me a long time to set priorities, to get an overview of everything I have on my plate. My whole life seems to be stuffed in my head, but I never go down to my legs. They're as far away to me as Antarctica. How did you know that, anyway?"

Taylor has told me how she sometimes feels like an alien among her peers, with their talk of jobs, children and careers. She feels more like an artist, someone who wants to create the world afresh and show that things can be different. When she talks, her hands flutter through the air like parakeets. Her arms flap up and down as if they have a life of their own, and aren't fully attached to her slender body. Without being in the least aware of it, she gives three clues that she drew this childhood conclusion at an early age: her feeling that she doesn't belong among people of her own age, her awareness of living mostly in her head and her loose flying limbs. These are all typical of people with a strong first childhood conclusion, who don't feel at home on the earth and prefer to stray off in their thoughts into more beautiful pastures. This straying tends to create challenges, with prodigious plans that never seem to come to fruition; and the challenge to organize daily life, be on time, get to all items on the to-do list without wandering off into no-man's-land.

Taylor is quick on the uptake. "Are you saying that I'd get more done if I would come down from the attic all the way to my legs? How do I do that?"

Growing up with this babyhood conclusion

For a decade, prize-winning *La La Land* director Damien Chazelle cherished a private dream. Inspired by the grand musical films of old, he wrote one, about a passionate jazz pianist and a gifted aspiring actress in present-day Los Angeles. Together with his former Harvard roommate, composer Justin Hurwitz, he kept his dream alive – and made it happen. With this nostalgic song-and-dance film he instantly became, as one interviewer said, "the most beloved man on earth." Does he still feel like he is in a dream? "Every time you get a chance to make a movie, it's like this miracle," the acclaimed young director responds, "and so I very consciously made this movie as if I would never make another one, because… who knows?"

Dreams are familiar territory for those of us with this very early childhood conclusion. Out of fear that we have no right to exist, we draw the energy up and out of our body and move to higher planes. We were the toddlers who gazed round-eyed at everything happening in kindergarten and, once at home, needed a lot of quiet time by ourselves to process the myriad impressions from our day. In the classroom, we couldn't stay focused as our thoughts would just fly away by themselves and take us with them to the fairy tales we had been read or fantasy places where we loved to dwell. When called back to the classroom, we couldn't help but dream, gazing out of the window again, quite soon. Yet, as if by magic we took everything in, because our boundaries are quite permeable and so all that is being said and done around us finds its way into our system. We are utterly sensitive and often understand how things work without needing it explained to us. Intuitively, we gave the right answers to questions that other kids struggled with.

Growing up, we continue to have trouble focusing on subjects that don't interest us immediately. We may zone out and before we know it time has passed and we are late and where have we left the car keys and where is the car parked anyway? The personification of the perplexed professor. Sometimes we are not even sure what we've been thinking about in our time away. We only know that it felt great to be hanging out wherever it was; it felt harmonious and peaceful, just the way we believe life on earth ought to be. Some of us, however, can name exactly where we were. We zoomed away from earth and were drifting among the planets. It might sound like a tall tale, but try asking a child with a faraway look in their eyes where they were. You'll be surprised. And they, in turn, will be surprised that anybody is asking them about the experiences that are so real to them and so foreign to people who don't walk this childhood conclusion's path.

Physical tells

With this childhood conclusion we build bodies like the airy cathedrals of old, constructed to stretch up high into the sky and get as close to God as humans could possibly reach. Often tall and lanky, we may feel like a lighthouse standing alone on an island far away from the shore in a vast sea. We look like one at times, when we have our eyes open wide and heads turning to see if we are safe here and now. Our eyes may have a frightened look, and we may find it difficult to focus just on one person in a conversation as our vision roams, both on the lookout for potential threat and to the spheres of inspiration.

It is also not unusual for us to have a hard time eating. The first unwelcoming sensations had us subtly shrink back from this corporal existence. Many of us don't really like these bodies that demand so much time for their upkeep. We find them cumbersome, slow and heavy compared to our fast-moving thoughts that can so clearly visualize new realities that we get impatient with the long time it takes to tend to our physical needs. We would rather be light. This makes us stall over supper and, once out from under our parents' supervision, tend to skip meals. Also, we are pernickety. We would rather not eat than take in something not to our liking.

Living half in and half out of the body is nothing out of the ordinary for us. Our frequent energetic upward movement leaves its tangible marks in that often one of our shoulders is higher than the other and the spine becomes slightly twisted, like a refined spiral staircase in a chic apartment building in one of the old boroughs of Paris. Our limbs appear to gain a life of their own. Without much coordination, they seem to move of their own volition as if they are not really attached to the torso. This leaves us awkward, and yet often inexplicably elegant at the same time.

Entering our body usually no further than the diaphragm, we are like a bust of the stately founder of the company in the entrance hall across from the elevators. Living only in the upper parts of the house, so to speak, has its disadvantages. Perennially cold hands and feet, for instance, as the upward energy is taken away from those extremities. We may sometimes feel we live in a fog as our vision is blurred from having our eye on space travel instead of on what is right in front of us. Our joints might be weak and our spiralling up and out of the body may bring back pain.

Overflowing with creative and original ideas as we are, we can become overexcited and hyperactive. Yet, we don't always find it easy to actually do anything with these ideas in any practical sense. We make a start, but then so many new visions come streaming in that we are immediately distracted as the new idea seems more attractive than the earlier ones.

At the end of the day we may be exhausted from all the impressions that have come flying into our system. We have no idea how other people shield themselves from the sensory overload of modern-day messages. We sense the feelings of people a mile away. An intense meeting or movie will leave us gaping with the sheer amount of information and sensations to be processed. Even a short train ride may have us in intense contact with the person across the aisle. Life is intense for those of us with this infanthood conclusion, so we need a lot of downtime to get ourselves together again.

Perfect or not

This babyhood conclusion often gives rise to a tendency towards perfection-ism – in other dimensions, we know, realms exist where harmony and beauty hold sway. The stubborn determination that it ought to be possible to realize that level of perfection down here can be crippling. We may become an artist with plans so ambitious that they just cannot be carried out. We may be the career woman who is constantly planning to move abroad but thinks of so many maybe's that it never happens. We may be the lover in a good and even long relationship who never quite commits, as commitment to one firm point is just not on our horizon. As soon as we picture life going on as it is now, we go into a panic as this, surely, is way too mundane. We feel suffocated, inhibited, a butterfly with its wings taken off; we will need to up and leave for greener fields where life may finally be as perfect as we have always imagined it could be.

However, when we reconcile ourselves to the slowness of atoms, molecules and other human beings, what comes out of our minds and hands will have originality and artistry. We are the designers of objects of the future. We make products that embody the spirit of the times. We demand good quality and will fight to maintain high standards. Our homes and offices are furnished sparsely and tastefully. In meetings, we may appear distracted, but seemingly out of the blue we can make observations that to the surprise of those around us are precisely to the point. We see connections that others have not fathomed. We are champions in brainstorming sessions as we can let inspiration run wild. Then, we are in our element. All seems perfect for a while.

Escape

Our lofty thoughts of being in the outer heavens let us escape from all sorts of difficult situations. We don't get involved in conflicts at work; *we* know better than to fight about mundane problems. Observing the superficial chatter of friends and colleagues, *we* are above such mindless drivel. We don't go into the question of how a plan must be financed; *we* aren't concerned with material matters.

When this early childhood conclusion's button is pushed, our heads explode with thoughts of better times future and past, of more peaceful places elsewhere – anything as long as we don't need to be where we are. The grass is so much greener on the other side, is what the looping thoughts would have us believe. This belief in a better world somewhere far away is not without its dangers.

As a child, Davy wrote poems and songs. With his long dark hair and big brown eyes, he was an enchanting boy who would spend hours sitting by himself in a corner with a thoughtful expression on his young face. His parents let him be, but they were shocked when one day he read them one of his poems. Why would a ten-year-old write about death? "Why not?" asked Davy, "we're all going to die, and maybe it isn't nearly as bad as we think."

Now Davy has turned 17 and he no longer writes. He no longer dares to give free rein to his imagination, and sometimes just sits alone for hours, staring into space. His parents have split up. His mother acts so jolly that he doesn't know what to say to her any more. Absorbed in his new wife and his new life, his father is only vaguely interested in his son these days. Davy no longer feels at ease with his friends, who are all into gadgets and girls. They seem obsessed with how they look, while Davy is searching for the meaning of life. His mates initially tell him to stop being so difficult, but soon give up and no longer ask him out with them.

Davy becomes more and more silent. He doesn't want to attend school any more and hides in his room, and in the question of whether life is worth living for him. He feels utterly alone but paradoxically, in that he is anything but alone. Thousands of others who feel the same way about the lack of meaning in the material yearn for a life of purpose. As long as we are ruled by thoughts that tell us we're not welcome, do not belong and had best leave – and all the other variations of this message that this childhood conclusion produces – life is no picnic.

It isn't hard to find ways to escape the harshness of this world: in books and films, on social media and the endless Internet, in the hazy daze of alcohol, cigarettes and drugs, into going out or working hard; in everything that numbs angst and anxiety, and allows an escape for a while from the cold hostile world. But it doesn't help. Not really.

Negative self-talk

When existential angst is triggered, thoughts that we are not welcome, or should not even exist, can hold us in a tight grip to the point of paralyzing us and preventing us from doing anything at all. This is the kind of endlessly repetitive self-talk that goes on when this primal childhood conclusion is active in us:

NEGATIVE SELF-TALK

I want to get away. Anywhere, as long as it isn't here.

The world is too coarse and brutal for me.

Something must surely have gone wrong somewhere.

I don't belong here.

My body is so awkward.

I don't know if I want to be in it.

I don't feel safe.

I need to go where it's quiet – harmonious, safe and light.

I belong somewhere else.

I know how life is meant to be.

Unlike most people, I'm not interested in material goods.

I am drawn to higher values, a spiritual life.

People don't understand how sensitive I am.

It is as if I pick up everybody else's feelings. I don't always know what to do with them – it's exhausting.

Modern life is just too busy and stressful for me.

I am not like other people, who don't even perceive the world I live in.

I wish I was a normal person with a normal life.

I just can't cope with all that is happening.

I want out, away from here.

I'm afraid.

I'd rather not be here.

Relentlessly recurring thought patterns like this make us antsy, flighty, not here, not there. We want to be present, but our runaway attention takes us forever out of here. We don't make eye contact in conversations, even if true human contact is what we yearn for. We also secretly feel that we are better than other people who don't live in outer space where we like to hang out. That is the fix we are in.

Core gifts

Every childhood conclusion is directly connected to the innate gifts we bring with us. It is exactly because of those mysterious inner qualities which we hold most dear that we responded so intensely to what transpired in our young life. We drew this childhood conclusion precisely because of the innate inclination towards aesthetics, sensitivity, spirituality and vision.

King Midas might have turned all that he touched into gold. With our high sense of aesthetics we turn all we touch into beauty. No need to explain Feng Shui to us as we instinctively know it. We will rearrange the furniture in a room or an office so it pleases the eye and calms the senses. We go to the shop in town that has the best flowers; after scrutinizing all of them we purchase a single one, which we put in a vase in a way that makes people look twice. Unmaterialistic as we are, we might not take an interest in fashion, but what we wear will be interesting, beautiful and of the highest quality we can afford. Beauty consoles us as it speaks directly to the soul. Aesthetics is one way for us to come close to perfection. We can make something from nothing. When we are happy, we light up like the sun and have everyone bask in our radiance.

A less sensitive person might have responded differently to their first rough treatment as a baby. They might have noticed, but not taken notice of it so deeply. Not us. With our exquisite sensitivity, we are open to signals that others don't pick up. We may want to close off a bit more at times, but unchecked these psychic antennae have us plugged into the inner workings of people near and far. As children, we feel the emotions of family members as intensely as our own. Later, as parents, we know what's going on with a child before they even enter the room. As colleagues and friends, the atmosphere in a space tells us what is going on underneath. As a result, we can often make instant deep contact.

With a strong inner sense of the indivisible oneness of all life, spirituality is to us what water is to a fish – a most natural habitat. Some of us cultivate this aspect of life through yoga, meditation or retreats with gurus in the Himalayas. Others have no need to go to spiritual centres as they themselves *are* one. Without studying books, poses or techniques, we live a life connected to higher realms of existence. If we have a religion or a spiritual preference, we may feel deep reverence for the sacred in all areas of life. Places where the ancients worshipped may affect us deeply, as we are in touch with the breath of life that connects us all.

A scout sees more from the mountaintop than from the valley down below. Us not wanting to incarnate fully may also have to do with the desire for vision, the longing to be able to see into the future as it could be formed. Transcending the obvious, we see the ideal over the horizon and can be strong visionary leaders with innovative ideas, flawless intuition and an unshakable trust in a better future.

Talents honed

As painful as the underlying early life experience was, and as distressing as the thoughts were that have harassed us ever since, the childhood conclusion set us on our way. The deduction we made as infants and children has directed us to develop certain innate qualities and leave others be.

In each of the companies he worked for, Jim was known for what is called a helicopter view: he can float above an organization, and without any previous knowledge somehow see how the processes work and how things can be organized more efficiently and effectively. Colleagues came to expect him to seem miles away only to snap out of his reverie at exactly the right moment and talk sense. They were mystified by the way he would put his finger on the raw spot. How could he know about the tension between departments where he rarely set foot? He must have a sixth sense, they agreed bemusedly.

All human beings have intuition, but we haven't all developed it, or rather some have left it undeveloped, in contrast to those of us who tend to soar high. Without a strong outer shield to ward off impressions, the inner compass of our intuition picks up signals whether we want it to or not. More than others we dare to give heed to what intuition tells us, and trust what we know without knowing how we know it. Deciding that a person is fully trustworthy, for instance, when in a country where we don't speak the language or know the culture, so our usual ways of gauging these things don't work. People with this early childhood conclusion tend to have incredible intuitive intelligence, as long as they don't allow it to be overshadowed by negative self-talk that causes them to doubt.

The existential paradox

Here we are with our precious gifts and yet with a strong sense that we actually shouldn't be here at all. This is the paradox that can trap us in this first childhood conclusion:

> **THE PARADOX**
>
> *If I daydream, I escape from the harshness of life but I can't achieve much. When I connect with the life in my body, then I am terrified of losing my higher self and be crushed.*

Part of the paradox is that the sensation of not belonging or needing to go elsewhere to find the perfect life is being kept alive by the dreaming. Living in a dream world in turn nurtures the notion that we will never truly belong or be understood and that anywhere else is better than where we are right now.

"I always feel like I got off the bus a stop too early," is how a high-level consultant described it to me the other day. The point is: as long as we listen to those thoughts that have us believe that we aren't welcome, that a mistake has been made in us being born here on this planet, that we don't belong, that it is better not to feel and feed the body and that we need to go elsewhere in order to find what we are looking for, we are reacting to what happened in the first hours or days of our life.

The challenge is to accept our existence. Many of us need to make the choice to live not once, but over and over again. Each time we opt for living, we incarnate a bit deeper, but it may take a while before we are fully here to stay.

Paradoxically, it is exactly through inhabiting our body that we will be able to live and manifest our exquisite gifts. We will have to engage with the fear of losing all that is precious to us when we incarnate. What may help is to change the imagery. We are not an elevator that travels the same route in a constricted channel all its working life, and when on the ground floor cannot open its doors on the seventh where, as we all know, the real exciting stuff happens. As human beings, we can be on all floors at the same time – our advantage over an elevator is that we can expand our energy field. The mind might not know what these words could possibly mean, but all of us naturally bring in our energy field when we are in a crowd or board a train so as not to have too much interference with others. The energy field itself knows how to contract and expand, so when we intend to expand it, it will. Spreading in the horizontal, we will also grow in the vertical and when we bring our centre of gravity slowly down, we may stay up in the ether and at the same time get a toe in the water of living on earth. We can be down to earth while not severing the connection to the higher realms of harmony and beauty.

The healing response

When we are overstimulated, hyperactive, out of our bodies, fixated on perfectionism and running the thought loop that everything would be way better if only we were somewhere else, we can give ourselves a healing response. This energetic work is much like putting on an oxygen mask and then helping others, as the flight attendants keep instructing us. Once we know how to give ourselves a healing response, we can give it to others.

First aid when we feel like a cat on hot bricks is to calm down by realizing what is going on. A childhood conclusion is playing up. We can quieten ourselves down by holding ourselves as we longed to be held when we were very little. Wrapping our arms around ourselves, we can hold ourselves, even rock ourselves a bit. No one will notice if we sit in a meeting or a café lightly stroking or softly patting our upper arms as if they were kittens. Inwardly we can repeat to ourselves that we are welcome, that it is good we have come to this earth, that we belong, that this very moment we are safe.

The physical sensation will help bring us down out of our overly busy head into the rest of our body. Then, taking our time, we can become conscious of where our energy is and start to bring it down. With the capacity of visualization as one of our bonus skills, we can imagine our energy field like a hot-air balloon that has accidentally gone up unmanned because somehow the weights came loose. It is floating upwards but the passengers have yet to get into the wicker basket. The balloon needs to be roped down so the navigator can get in and give direction to the flight of the day. Life works better when our energy field doesn't float about freely but extends all the way to the ground. We will feel better when we dwell in all of our body instead of only the upper part, or even, as many of us do, only our head.

Moving the energy down starts with climbing up to the highest point we can reach, tuning in to how it feels like home and making an internal promise not to leave it as we explore what lies beneath. Like coming down from a high mountaintop, the first stop is inside our head where we can visualize calmness in our busy brain, relaxation of our vigilant eyes. We can move our jaws to relax muscles that have tightened up, make funny faces, stick out our tongue until an involuntary smile appears on our lips. Then we move down to the throat. When it is constricted, we can visualize it relaxing, widening, opening so the energy can flow through like molasses. At the level of the heart, a warmth can spread throughout our torso and into the arms. The diaphragm might give us some trouble, being a boundary that we seldom cross; but once the torso is filled with warm energy, the diaphragm might not feel as stiff as previously and we might pass it more easily than we thought we could as, still visualizing and noticing the effects in our bodies, we allow the energy to move through our stomach and abdomen, down towards the sacrum and sexual organs, further down still into the upper legs, lower legs, feet – all the way down to the ground. We may feel tingly and warm all over. The more often we practise this exercise that helps us come down to earth, the easier it becomes to live in all of the 30 trillion cells that miraculously make up the body. Maybe incarnation isn't so bad, after all.

Once we know how to bring ourselves down to earth, we can begin to help others when we see them go up and out of their bodies. Consciously going up there to meet them without losing our own grounding, we can assist them in coming down again, slowly from one level to the next, spending time at each station until the train is ready to move further down again. We can radiate out to them that they are welcome, that they belong and that right now it is safe for them to be here.

Repeating the assurance that we are welcome and practising this energetic healing response will help all of us to be grounded in that place of inner peace from which everything is possible. Moving into the whole of our bodies instead of living only on the upper floors will give us a new lease of life; using the untapped capacities of our bodies as a whole can allow us to bring so much more to the table.

Turning this childhood conclusion

The energetic healing response is highly effective. It may benefit from being complemented by a more verbal approach. Turning a childhood conclusion helps transform our unhelpful jittery thoughts, as we acknowledge and feel the underlying emotions so they can dissolve. Once we realize that the looping thoughts that make us believe we aren't welcome and don't belong keep us from fully bringing our gifts to life, we can start to do something about it. Here's a concise description of the five steps.

STEP 1: recognize this thought pattern

When the familiar anxiety that we are not welcome, don't belong and need to get away makes us fidget and fret, the first step is to recognize this complex of thought and feelings. Seeing the pattern, we learn that all of these jiggles and jitters arise from a conclusion we drew in the first minutes, hours or days of our life.

STEP 2: shift the focus

We next bring the focus to the present, to who we have become. As we feel our growth, the resilience with which we have survived everything up until now, we become aware of our unique gifts and extraordinary potential.

39

STEP 3: thank ourselves

The alarm of being unwelcome and all the accompanying thoughts spring from a traumatic experience around the time of our birth. This childhood conclusion has offered us the possibility of escape. Now we may thank this part of us that, with the perspective of a newborn, took the up, up and away motion to be the best possible option.

STEP 4: invite the terror from back then

As the adult we are now, we consciously invite the terror we felt then to come up as we hold it. We will feel the panic that we are one of nature's mistakes, that we don't belong here, that we aren't welcome – and let it flow through us. The intensity of it will last no more than a few minutes. Then we'll be through it. We'll still be alive.

STEP 5: welcome our existence on earth

We can breathe a sigh of relief now. We felt our deepest fear, this very human fear of death, fear of life, fear of severing the connection to spirit. Coming out the other end brings us here more – and brings more of us here. We are welcome.

Turning our thoughts

"You're welcome". What a wonderful phrase that is, and it's being said without thinking millions of times a day. What if we started to take this standard response for what it actually means? It is exactly what we need to integrate: that we are welcome, with our strengths and weaknesses, our doubts and fears, thoughts and feelings, our inspired approach and our intuitive flashes. We are welcome the way we are. Just like everybody.

More than half the people who used to come to my private practice – young and old, men and women, seekers and career workers – had questions related to this first childhood conclusion. They felt different from their friends, permanently restless, never really comfortable anywhere as if they'd accidentally landed here while on their way to another planet. They felt butterflies in their stomach, collywobbles, the jitters, the willies, the heebie-jeebies, the shakes, the screaming abdabs, the jumps, the jim-jams, the yips. The fact that the English language has so many highly descriptive words for this state may be a pointer that many more of us than we tend to think are familiar with these feelings.

I do not claim that turning the childhood conclusion is the magic fix-it-all. A youngster like Davy will probably need more guidance in order to be able to get back into his life. My friend Jim had done a good measure of self-reflection before the penny dropped that he was welcome. When it did, he laughed and laughed. He couldn't believe he had never seen his thoughts for what they were: painful reminders of pain he had wanted to avoid. "What a joke," he said, once he had started to feel like a whole person for the first time in his life. "God must have a peculiar sense of humour that he sends people out for decades to escape what has never been there in the first place."

Turning the childhood conclusion provides some distance between ourselves and our stream of thoughts. As with everything practice is the key, and this practice begins with watching our thoughts instead of accepting them for real. We're often so used to believing what we think that we may need to remind ourselves often that we can simply register thoughts without necessarily attaching any value to them.

Turning this very young childhood conclusion is a useful exercise to repeat over and over again. Patience is a good companion on this journey. Rewiring ourselves and learning new habits to replace the old is not done overnight. Fortunately, it can be done unobtrusively. If the jitters hit us while we are on the way to work, or in the office, we can get them to subside with just the first three steps of the method. When we have more time, or if we notice that this childhood conclusion regularly takes us for a ride, we can intervene more radically by going through all five steps.

The first three steps

The first three steps of turning the childhood conclusion can be done any time and anywhere. Nobody else needs notice a thing as we recognize and thank our escapist inclination and return our attention to who we are now.

STEP 1: recognize the thought pattern

The first step towards a more peaceful and embodied existence is to become aware of our feelings and thoughts. Since we are not our thoughts, but we have them, we can look at them. Those of us who meditate regularly or practise mindfulness will already be trained to watch our thoughts and feelings like clouds in the sky that come and go. Others might want to begin this new practice by installing a "virtual camera" that records our thoughts so we can observe them without rushing along with them. Practice will pay off, especially at moments when we feel panic rising or when we overreact to something or someone. This first step is about cultivating the presence of mind to watch our flighty feelings and thoughts. Once we see them come back again and again, we will begin to be able to recognize these reactions as having their origin in impressions formed when we had only just been born.

STEP 2: shift the focus

We are no longer the hapless baby who fully depended on parents or carers. Whatever has happened – our childhood, school years, puberty with all its ups and downs, the sorrows of love, perhaps the separation of our parents, the loss of someone dear – we have withstood it. When we stop to think about it, we can perhaps conclude that we are much stronger than we give ourselves credit for. What's more, there are people to whom we are important. Nobody else is put together quite like us, and we have something unique to offer the world. Pondering on what we have learned so far, we may stand tall.

STEP 3: thank ourselves

This childhood conclusion has allowed us to develop our intuition, our natural connection to the world of ideas and of spirit, our sense of beauty, our sensitivity to atmosphere, our originality and inventiveness and our helicopter view. There is no better time than this very moment to start appreciating what this babyhood conclusion has done for us. Even if we're sitting on the Underground, or having a quick coffee, giving thanks can be done in silence and need not take long. We may even thank all the rattling negative self-talk that has seen us seek new territory out of a sense of not belonging where we were. Expressing gratitude means we will no longer fight the tendency to dream or be enraged about the brutality and imperfection of life. We only have to say thank you. This step is a sure-fire way to calm our thoughts.

Fully turning this childhood conclusion

Going through the first three steps of turning this early childhood conclusion is the on-the-go version. Being grounded more firmly in a positive present needs deeper diving. This next step has us engage with the terror that we have held from our earliest days by seeking it out and letting it move through us, so we can feel welcome and alive.

STEP 4: invite the fear from back then

In this step as the adult we have become, we hold space for some of our very early feelings of existential terror. We begin by consciously choosing to feel good about ourselves as the adult who has grown out of the tiny baby we once were. Aware of our gifts and how we have developed them, we can now travel back through our memories to a moment when we felt a ferocious fear. It could be quite recent or a while ago, as long as it is a moment when our heart was pounding with panic or when anxiety had us by the throat. Maybe we know why; maybe it happened for no clear reason. As the person we are now, we can deliberately evoke that alarm and panic again. Sometimes it helps to close the eyes to call up the situation and get back into the fear we are intentionally revisiting. The aim is not to get lost in it, so a small dose of anxiety is enough, as long as we feel it. Then we can let this fear move through the body, noticing sensations, images, travelling pains in our chest, throat and head. Our breath may be quickening, or maybe we're holding it. If so, then it is good to take a deliberate breath as we don't want anything to get stuck right now; we want to feel the panic so we can let it move through us and dissipate. We breathe through the pain and panic, all the time realizing that we have grown up. We are no longer the infant we were.

Not only can we experience the fright from then, we can also look at it in order to release it. Enduring just a bit longer, keep going... until we feel the pain or fear recede. It will happen. It always does – our unwelcome self-image is based in an illusion and thus has no energy to sustain itself once it is recognized for what it is: a big conclusion we drew when we were very little. Right here, right now, we are safe. Nothing untoward is happening this second. Once we've gone to the depths of what we most feared and have survived, we will feel lighter and at the same time more grounded. This may be a good time to glance in a mirror and radiate out to ourselves that we are welcome. We will be no exception if we burst out laughing. That's just a sign that it has worked.

STEP 5: live our life on earth

Here we are, alive and kicking and just as welcome as everybody else. The more grounded we become, the more grace we will find in daily life. When we become more present in what we are doing, we will also find it easier to be in contact with others and not let them frighten us off into the safe land of dreams with a remark made in passing. We will no longer feel like the odd one out, a lost sheep. That was what our single-minded thoughts had made us out to be, but it's no longer necessary to keep up this self-image and all the stories that go with it. We can replace this image with another, one that works for us. For instance, that we are a gifted spirited person. Together with our sensitivity and wealth of ideas, our helicopter vision will help us move forward. Once we're over the fear, we will be able to marshal our gifts from our inspiring visions and idealism to our sense of harmony, beauty and good proportions. Thank heavens. We are welcome.

A positive present

After my book in Dutch on the childhood conclusions came out in 2011, my colleague and friend Anne-Marie Voorhoeve started to put the insights into practice straight away. She did this in her work as co-founder of The Hague Center for Global Governance, Innovation and Emergence as well as at home. While in a meeting with her at her house in the country with a lake on each side, I witnessed how she responded when we heard the clatter of pots and lids crashing from a kitchen cupboard. "My daughter planned to bake a banana cake," she said to me. Then, in the direction of the kitchen, she called: "Ground down, remember? Visualize a strong connection between your feet and the earth." We heard her young daughter heave a big sigh. A minute of total silence later, she must have been piling the pots back into the cupboard. A lid slipped off again. "Try harder," my friend called. "I'm welllllllllllllcome!" came back from the kitchen. "Yes, you are!" her mother sang, and with a wink to me, "you are very, very welcome." After a while we heard humming as the teenager went about her baking. Of course, she had rolled her eyes and thought her mother was bonkers. She also came in later, however, to share how she had grounded down some more before getting the flour out, just to be on the safe side.

When we practise turning this childhood conclusion regularly, we will notice that negative thoughts gradually lose their strength and thus their power over us. We will become aware that we start to respond differently to situations that used to make us feel awkward and estranged. We will be able to stay present where once we disappeared. We will be able to finish what we started. At some point, we will become able to recognize a negative thought and replace it with a positive one straight away. What we concluded as a baby does not necessarily hold water. We may just as well think the opposite. Better, actually, because positive thoughts like the ones below make us feel relaxed, at home and happy:

POSITIVE SELF-TALK

I am welcome.
I belong, and I belong here.
I don't have to be afraid, because nothing can happen to me.
I am at peace with life on earth, no matter how hard it is.
I trust that it is good that I was born, no matter how imperfect
    life may be.
There is also much beauty in the world. In nature, in art, in love.
I am choosy, and I permit myself to be.
I love beautiful things and I like to surround myself with them.
I know that my body is vulnerable, but I am not my body.
I am and will always be a divine creation of consciousness.
In reality, nothing can harm me.
I don't have to run away any more.
It makes no difference where I am.
Wherever I am, is good.
It is good here.
I can be here.
I am safe.
I am welcome, with my intuition, my sensitivity and my depth,
    with my lightness and my drive to leave the world better
    than I found it.
I am a member of the human race.
Just like everybody else.

Dance through life

Dancer and choreographer Martha Graham single-handedly turned old-fashioned ballet into 20th-century dance. "The body says what words cannot. Nothing is more revealing than movement," she famously said. As we inhabit our bodies more fully, we will retain an open connection to the realm of ideas and of spirit while being able to navigate the much slower material world with more patience and endurance. Our bodies will feel better, not just as elegant garments but as a house we like to live in, or if you like, a temple we inhabit for as long as it lasts.

Martha Graham put it like this to a younger friend, a fabulous dancer who doubted her talent: "There is a vitality, a life force, an energy, a quickening that is translated through you into action, and because there is only one of you in all of time, this expression is unique. If you block it, it will never exist through any other medium and the world will not have it. It is not your business to determine how good it is nor how valuable nor how it compares with other expressions. It is your business to keep yourself open and aware to the urges that motivate you. Keep the channel open."

Once we have our feet underneath us and believe that who we are and what we have to offer is valuable, we will see the world with new eyes. We are interested in spiritual matters and can work wonders when we see purpose and meaning in our actions. We intuitively understand children, clients and friends. We see the potential of spaces, interiors and atmosphere, of novel ideas and innovative thinkers. We continue to be able to travel to the stars and revive ourselves in the world of spirit, inspiration and fantasy. Sometimes it seems to others as if we can see into the future. Most important of all is that we come to know and acknowledge deeply that who we are and what we bring to the dancefloor is welcome – that we welcome our existence as we are welcome to it.

2

Living to give

"There isn't enough, I am not enough."

NEGATIVE SELF-TALK

"I am not good enough. I am not attentive, critical, determined, efficient, funny, generous, good-looking, kind, positive, tall, thin, well-educated enough. There is never enough time."

CORE GIFTS

abundance, curiosity, generosity, vivacity

In the 90s, I had a firm specializing in internal corporate communication and my team and I were fortunate enough to count among our clients a number of large global players. I loved working for these big organizations with their intricate communication issues and their insistence on high quality. Bigger agencies in our line of work would ask these multinationals why in heaven's name they worked with our small outfit. I was super-proud of my highly intelligent and articulate team.

They, however, had to cover for me as sometimes I became undone. Even at that time, the head offices of our big-firm clients had elaborate procedures for those who wished to enter their fortress. Identifying ourselves first at the entrance to the car park, again at the elevator and once more at the reception desk, only to be told to sit and wait while they rang for someone to come and collect us, never failed to make me distraught. By the time an eager assistant came for us, more often than not I was on the verge of crying. New colleagues would look at me askance, wondering what was going on with their boss who was usually so composed. Others knew they would have to step in and make the small talk in the elevator while I tried to regain my composure. Familiar with my antics or not, they also raised their eyebrows behind the client's back, the unspoken message being: "What has got into you?" or "Can you pull yourself together, please?"

The few minutes' wait often had me in such distress that I couldn't even take the lead in presenting our work in the meeting. My colleagues had to take over as if nothing was the matter while I kept fighting back my tears and trying to calm down. If I spoke at all in the first half hour, everyone around the meeting table could hear the tremor that I tried to keep out of my voice.

It was highly embarrassing and it happened in other places, too. In queues of any kind I would quickly grow impatient, to the point of being rude to the people behind the counter. I marched out of the hairdresser's when I was on time for my appointment and, not yet ready, they kept me standing at the counter. I once threw a bra – fortunately this is quite some time ago now – at a store assistant when she said I was too late bringing it back and I couldn't change it. Shouting over my shoulder as I stormed out that this was no way to treat a good customer and that I would never again shop in their store, I felt fully entitled to my indignation. At the same time, I was at sea as to what came over me.

I felt ashamed of these involuntary impulsive actions and prayed people wouldn't notice, but bystanders, friends and boyfriends of course wondered at these sudden outbursts. I apologized, begged pardon, offered my excuses, saying that this was not at all how I wanted to be, let alone treat other people. Yet, whenever I was kept waiting, within a few minutes I would be at the point of boiling over with impatience and rage, and I often spoke out sharply, demanding attention.

Good people behaving badly

This might all sound a bit dramatic, and I wish I was exaggerating, but I am not. One consolation is that I am not the only one who flips when being kept waiting at the counter or getting stuck in a traffic jam. A good many of us, while in general being generous, gregarious, fun people to be with, are not on our best behaviour when waiting in queues. Somehow, we cannot curb the tendency to sound aggrieved, querulous and self-righteous once it finally is our turn.

What came over me in such situations remained a complete and utter mystery for years. I tried what I could to program myself differently but nothing really worked until I discovered the childhood conclusions fix. Seeing my incomprehensible deportment described as typical for someone who has drawn the childhood conclusion "There isn't enough, I am not enough", a weight fell from my shoulders. It came as a huge relief to understand that the adult me was thrown off balance by having to wait because of babyhood terror of being left to my own devices.

As babies, we are fully dependent for our survival on the care of others and so we suffer agonies when we wake up hungry and no one comes to feed, clean and hold us. I immediately recognized this alarmed state of the baby I once was in the consternation I felt as an adult each time I had to wait. Belatedly, I would like to apologize to all whom I have treated unkindly as a consequence of that early state of consternation. I behaved like a child. I own up to that now and through working with this childhood conclusion, these days I can happily wait my turn.

The recurring thought patterns that are generated by this childhood conclusion are typically ones with which we undermine ourselves, our relationships with others and thus, our fulfilment. A baby needs an enormous amount of care. This seemingly unappeasable need of the infant we once were is still at work in us as adults. The end of this chapter again presents a healing response as well as the five steps to turn this childhood conclusion. We have the means of stilling these "not enough" thoughts about ourselves and becoming whole. Because we *are* enough. We may always strive to be better tomorrow than we are today; being human is being constantly in flux – we take on and integrate new information all the time. In essence, however, right now we are enough right as we are. Everyone is.

The origin of this childhood conclusion

The classic event at the root of the "There isn't enough, I am not enough" childhood conclusion goes something like this. The baby wakes out of hunger. It makes small noises to alert its mother – or anyone else who is capable of bringing the nourishment the infant needs for its survival and growth. When no one comes, the baby begins to whimper, then to cry, and finally to scream with anguish. It kicks its legs and stretches out its arms in an attempt to attract the attention of anyone who might be looking on from a distance, spending a lot of precious energy in the process. Without any sense of time the small creature works itself into a frenzy, its little face red from the effort and the exhaustion. The wee body that is so incredibly busy growing needs a fresh energy boost, and needs it NOW! The infant's system goes into overdrive as it instinctively fears for its survival as a lone creature in a world where no one seems to care whether it lives or not.

The mother has a timetable of her own or is busy doing something else. Nor is the father or another carer able to go to the child within minutes of it waking up. There may be hundreds of perfectly plausible reasons for why parents don't come instantly when their little one cries. Yet, while *they* know that it won't be too long, and that the child will get what it needs in good time, the baby doesn't know any of that. All it registers is that there is nobody around to give it what it so urgently needs right now. It summons up all its strength for one more squawk, one more desperate wave of the tiny arms, and then it's out of energy. It lets its arms fall and with them falls the small child's confidence in its environment. No one has come, perhaps no one ever will – that is the discouraging conclusion silently and unconsciously reached. In the experience of a child who has as yet no conception of time, this could easily be the end.

Parents compromise

Parents, even those gifted with an angel's patience, know how trying it is to look after an infant's every need. After the birth of her first child and while pregnant with the second, novelist Rachel Cusk wrote *A Life's Work: On Becoming a Mother*. She describes herself being taken by surprise at the exhaustive amount of care her daughter required. "There is in truth no utterance that could express the magnitude of the change from woman or man to mother or father," she writes in this controversial book that is both a very personal and a highly impersonal account of modern-day motherhood. "It is like a social experiment, something a scientist would do: leave a baby in a room with two adults, retreat, and see what happens. The baby cries. The woman picks up the baby. The sound stops. When she tries to put it down again the baby cries. She holds it for a long time. The man grows bored and the woman tries to put the baby down but it cries. The man walks around with it and it stops. The man grows tired. Both the man and the woman sit down and look at the baby anxiously." Her portrayal of getting the baby to sleep, feeding it every three hours for a year, the endless nappies, paints not a rosy picture of the enormous task parents, especially mothers, embark upon.

At the other end of the spectrum are those who see parenthood as a sacred commitment. In that light every moment, from changing nappies to cleaning up after the tot has thrown its plate of mashed carrots to the floor, is an opportunity to expand their love and their capacity to be patient and caring. Embracing the constant challenges of parenthood, through this approach, becomes a continual practice of mindful living. A young couple I know resolved never to have their baby daughter feel uncared for. One of them was always with her. If she could not sleep one of them would walk around with her for hours, if needed, night after night.

Most parents, however, will find themselves somewhere in between these two styles. They are constantly compromising as other children claim their attention and next day's work needs them fresh and able to concentrate. While doing their best, they will not always be able or willing to give their offspring exactly what it needs exactly when it needs it.

A good many of us have turned the effect of not being fed when we needed to be, or held and cuddled enough when we yearned for more intimate contact, into a belief that we ourselves are not enough. This is how the second childhood conclusion is born, the one that whispers continually in the ear of many of us that we are not sociable, strong, smart, attractive, amiable, helpful,

intelligent, fashionable, fast, firm, competent, compassionate, easy-going, ro-
mantic, up-to-date, laptop-literate, learned, liked, determined, grateful, gra-
cious, gallant, deep, appreciative, popular, responsible, connective, connected, careful – or whatever – enough. It's enough to drive us nuts sometimes.

My story continued

Back to my own history. I was born in 1954 and Dr Benjamin Spock's revolutionary book *Baby and Child Care* had been a best-seller since its publication
in 1946. His handbook gave – and in its revised 65th anniversary edition
still gives – expert advice on everything from equipment for bathing and the
decision on breast or formula to talking with teens about sex. The book was
dubbed revolutionary at the time, because this paediatrician saw a child as
an individual and was of the opinion that mothers knew very well what was
best for their own child. Spock also countered the popular belief that parents
would spoil their children by catering to their every need. "Young infants can't
anticipate the future," he wrote. "They live entirely in the here and now. They
also cannot formulate the thought 'I'm going to make life miserable for these
people until they give me everything I want.' What infants are learning during this first period is a sense of basic trust in the world. If their needs are met
promptly and lovingly, they come to feel that good things generally happen."

When I found out about the far-reaching influence of our childhood conclusions and realized how much I was still run by the constricting anguish
produced in me by this one, I asked my mother about my early days. What
were her and my father's ideas on rearing a child? She knew of the famous Dr
Spock, of course. Everybody in their circle of friends at the time, she said, was
talking about his approach that was so contrary to the golden rule of "rest,
cleanliness and regularity" that had been the rigid norm so far. True post-war
people, my parents and their friends were excited to rebuild society and raise
their children to be happy citizens in a modern way. The maternity nurse,
however, who came to instruct my mother was not at all taken in by these
new-fangled ideas and so she sternly advised my mother to leave me crying in
my crib until the regulated time of feeding.

"It was dreadful!" my mother remembers with regret. "All I wanted was to pick you up, hold you and feed you, but it wasn't allowed. I thought I was doing the right thing by restraining myself and not doing what I would have most loved to do." Intending to do what was best for me, my mother instead kept obediently to the routine prescribed by the medical authorities. With the three siblings who were to follow, she knew better. She followed her own counsel, with Dr Spock's handbook always within easy reach. With me, however, she was a first-time mother. Out of insecurity she resolved to do the best she could for me by listening to the experienced nurse, even this meant denying herself the pleasure of spending as much time with me as she wanted. When I cried in my crib, she would grip the arms of the chair she was sitting in tightly to stop herself from going in and comforting me. When the implacable clock finally gave her permission to go fetch me, she would feel terrible when she found me in distress. I must already have drawn a conclusion that would mark me for life – both negatively and positively as this conviction also lays the groundwork for the vivacious qualities we go on to develop.

One conclusion, two directions

This second childhood conclusion makes for lively, curious children who always have one more question to ask in order to satisfy their endless appetite. Many of us develop into engaging adults with a wide range of interests. We can never have enough friends, read enough blogs or see enough films. Some of us like to discuss what happens in our lives and in the world at large, at great length. At parties, we stay late as we don't want to miss anything. Never a dull moment with one of us in the room. That is how we look to the outside world, anyway. The inner experience may be very different as our thoughts keep reminding us that whatever we do, we will never be enough.

This conviction of not having or being enough pushes children to progress in one of two directions: towards a certain neediness, or just the opposite, towards fierce independence. This may even happen in the same family, as is shown by Sonia, who is full of disdain after visiting her sister. "She bought us all these over-the-top presents. I find it ridiculous for my children to wear designer labels, but my sister thinks I dress them in rags. She always sports the latest from the most expensive brands she can find. Her closets are filled to the brink with shoes and handbags that she says I'm welcome to have, because they're last year's. I don't want any of her gear. I need none of her hand-me-downs. Life surely must be about more than collecting stuff! It seems as if my sister is never satisfied with what she has, while I don't need anything much at all – or anyone, for that matter."

Two sisters, two souls, one childhood conclusion. With their common feeling of insufficiency, these two siblings set out in opposite directions. Where one compensates by exaggerating a material lifestyle, the other does so by minimizing and seemingly not needing anything. Their interactions are charged as each of them tries to convince the other that her way of life is surely best. Sonia is inclined to look down her nose a bit and consider herself a better person than her sister, whom she finds superficial, with her shopping mania. Simultaneously her sister tends to look down on Sonia, whom she considers out of touch with reality in her stubborn simplicity. In the meantime, below the surface still vying for the place of who is their parents' favourite daughter, the sisters do not give each other the affection and friendship they both long for.

Growing up with this childhood conclusion

Many of us will have either read to our own children or been read *The Very Hungry Caterpillar*. This sweet book that Eric Carle created almost half a century ago is reportedly still selling a copy a minute somewhere around the globe. It's one of those stories that can never be gone through often enough for a child. When the caterpillar has eaten its one apple, two pears, three plums… all the way to the fresh green leaf, spun itself into a cocoon and made its magical reappearance as a beautiful butterfly, it must be read from the beginning again. And once more. And then some, and as little as we are we will whine, cajole and nag until we get our way.

Typically, these children will always clamour for one more biscuit, one more game, one minute later to bed, one more story, one more kiss, one more confirmation that our parents are *really* there, *really* love us, *really, really,*

55

really. Can they say it one more time, please? Then we will have enough. We promise. Only it doesn't work that way; the insatiable need for confirmation raises its head as soon as the light is out.

We find creative ways to keep our parents' or carers' attention for as long as possible. We spin a lively story that goes on and on, so that parents will stay sitting on the edge of the bed, all their attention on us. At a family get-together, we will be ready to perform in front of everyone and revel in being in the spotlight. We get high grades in order to earn our parents' approval. If we can't grab their recognition that way, we will make them give it to us by being naughty and behaving badly. One way or the other, we need their eyes on us, we need their time and attention, we need them to fill this hole inside of us that we seem to be at the mercy of.

Alas, however much attention we are being given, it never really helps as the good feeling we momentarily get seems to melt away quickly. "Is it never enough for you?" parents sometimes cry out in despair. For children with a needy wiring, the answer unfortunately seems to be "No, it's never enough!"

In truth, no one can fill the hole of this neediness but us, we ourselves, once we begin to replace the distressed thoughts of need with the affirmation "I am enough, not too much, not too little, exactly enough" and begin to lay a bottom in that pit.

Fiercely independent

On the basis of feeling we can't rely on anyone, this childhood conclusion can also make us strive for total and utter independence from a very early age. We will, for instance, start walking very early. "Look at our little one," the proud parents gloat. They are often unaware that their prodigy is mainly eager to be able to walk so they can, so to speak, walk away from them. Inner determination has the child want to stand on their own two feet at the earliest possible moment, because being dependent on others for survival has turned out to be a terrifying experience. Instinctively we would rather not put our fortune into other people's hands any longer, because we never know if we really can count on them. Sometimes they show up, sometimes they don't. There's no way of telling. Somewhere in our young child's brain we conclude that it's crucial for our well-being to be able to do everything for ourselves as quickly as we can.

With this independent spirit we make life easy for our parents as they don't have to watch out for us much. We can soon bathe and dress ourselves. When off to visit Grandma, we will be sitting ready in the car, and yes, we have gone to the bathroom. Later, when leaving on holiday, we think ahead about what we will need at our destination so we won't get into a situation where we will have to ask for anything that we could have brought. When it rains, we would rather come home drenched through than borrow a rain jacket or an umbrella from a friend. Never mind us. We will be all right. We make do. We don't need a thing from anybody. We are fine. Don't you worry.

From a child that strives for maximum independence out of feelings of abandonment, we will grow into adults who simply can't and won't ask for help. Ever. Not us. We simply cannot bring ourselves to depend on someone else, or owe someone a favour. Not that we are unwilling to lend a hand. Quite the contrary – we tend to go out of our way for others, still convinced we haven't done enough, but ask someone else to do even the smallest thing for us? No thanks! Truth is, we find that way too scary.

Feeling (a) disappointment

As hard as it is for a parent to fulfil the needs of a demanding baby, to many of us it seems equally hard to fulfil our parents' expectations. Fed by the unrelenting thought patterns generated by this needy childhood conclusion, many of us tend to harbour a sense of disappointment. The line between nursing a sense of disappointment in others and feeling like a disappointment ourselves can be very fine, as the story of Giselle shows.

"Are you working hard enough? Are you earning enough?" Telephone conversations between Giselle and her father always begin with the same questions. "Yes, Dad. You really don't have to worry about me. The business is going well, I am doing well. Today I'm going shopping." Giselle loves her work at a popular florist's. She enjoys pointing people to flowers that are in season and she has a good eye for what works in a bouquet. Provided she doesn't go out too often, she makes ends meet on her monthly salary and can even afford the occasional shopping spree. She is content with her life, but it seems as if her father always expects more from her. As if she always manages to disappoint him in one way or another, no matter how much she tries to do her best.

The call makes Giselle feel like a little girl again, one who will never be good enough. Will her father ever be satisfied with her? She is disappointed that he doesn't see how exceptional it is that she got this job in the first place. After the call she continues to talk to her dad in her mind. "Do you even know how many people applied for this job?" her indignant thoughts repeat over and over. "You should be proud of me, instead of leaving me with the impression that I'm not doing well enough for your high and mighty standards!"

Giselle could just burst out crying, all by her lonesome self. "Nothing I do is good enough," she thinks sadly. "Of course, I don't have a boyfriend either." She hangs her head, lets her shoulders droop and bites her nails. Dissatisfied suddenly with herself and her life, all desire to go shopping has vanished. She shrugs and thinks that she has enough clothes in her closet already – too many to wear. Or maybe she would feel better if she bought something new, she considers. But she just doesn't have the energy so she settles on the sofa and watches a movie she has seen before, in a half-hearted attempt still to have a good enough day off.

Lack of self-confidence

Under stress our fierce independence might prove not as strong as it looks. We may collapse into lack of self-confidence with the inner voice constantly questioning: are we really nice, smart or cool enough? Self-pity holds no secrets for us, when we land in this aspect of this childhood conclusion; nor do complaining, moaning, fretting and whining or feeling – and sometimes even acting – as if we are helpless. We find it hard, even once we are older, when someone gets a bigger piece of the pie, a larger room, a better place at the table. We can react out of all proportion, even as adults, when we feel we are not served fast enough in a restaurant or paid enough attention to or haven't received a big enough portion for our money. When someone pushes ahead in a queue, without giving it a minute's thought our instant reaction is to speak up sharply – for some even to the point of wanting to get physical. Such vehemence is not always in line with the self-image of someone who needs to be cared for and catered to, but insight into the origin of this childhood conclusion brings understanding. Such unreasonable conduct harks back to a time when reason was not an option. When the baby had to eat. NOW!

Negative self-talk

Good enough or not, we soldier on. Others may regard us as capable and proficient people but the internal experience can be very different, as is the case with Luis, who serves on the board of a primary school. He was invited because he is never above stepping in when he sees a situation where help is needed. Moreover, he is someone who is happy to state clearly where he sees room for improvement. The voluntary post he accepted with such pleasure has soon become a torment, though, as griping thoughts increasingly torment him, "I know nothing about running a school. I haven't been shown the ropes by anyone. How can I find out what I need to know? Why did I even step into this position of responsibility?" Seen from the outside, he is the same capable and engaging man who makes sensible comments, but inside he is yammering like a child. "Could they just be too polite to tell me I'm a disappointment in this post? I want to go back to being just one of the parents. Then I can say what I think without having to bear the brunt. I will just force their hand and they will have to let me go. I know I'm just not good enough."

The insecurity about never quite making the mark has us on edge a lot of the time. We can tell when the childhood conclusion "There isn't enough, I am not enough" is triggered when we are haunted by ongoing inner lamentations like:

NEGATIVE SELF-TALK

I am not kind/considerate/liked/good-looking/smart enough.
I don't have enough time to do everything I need to do.
Only if I work really hard will I be appreciated.
No one must know that I am not up to the task.
I always give what I can, but it will probably not be enough.
Nobody does as much for others as I do.
I always have to do everything by myself.
People will leave me waiting for support until the cows come home.
No one ever keeps their appointments but me.
I'd better never count on anybody.
I won't need.
I will only be disappointed.
There is nobody who really cares about me.
I refuse to ask for what I need.
If I have to ask, I can never be sure that people value me.
I'm probably a disappointment myself.
I feel lonely and sad.
I suppose I'll just do it alone, like I always do.
If only I can do this well enough…

The eyes become sad, the head starts to hang, the shoulders droop, the breast caves in, the step gets heavy. We may never have shared this inner groaning with others, but rather kept the secret of our inadequacy to ourselves. Truth is, innumerable people think that they can never do enough, have been dealt the wrong hand, can't depend on anybody and end up carrying the world on their shoulders. They may also be telling themselves inwardly over and over again that they are always the one giving and giving, never receiving anything much back.

Those of us who lend our ears easily to such ongoing thoughts of dissatisfaction will not even notice the appreciation that comes our way. We might get into the habit of complaining about everything and everyone, to the point that people end up avoiding us. Then we sigh and say "See, I'm not good enough company."

The "not-enough" thought is like a piece of Velcro that can attach itself to anything. We don't do enough, we don't have enough, we will never be enough. That, however, is a warped self-image that is grounded in unfortunate early-life experiences, but not in the truth. In essence we are all enough – and we have a plethora of gifts that the not-enough thoughts keep us from presenting.

Core gifts

Abundance seems a strange gift for those of us obsessed with not having or being enough, but there you have it. We responded so vehemently to the lack of care and comforting in our early days precisely because we are creatures to whom the abundance of life, light and love come naturally. Once we relax into enoughness on this earth plane, we will find our inner abundance again. We will be so full of ourselves, in the very best sense of the word, that we will overflow. As Oprah Winfrey said when she was interviewed by Brené Brown to kick off her *Living Brave* series, "I work at being full. I want to be so full, I am overflowing, so 'when you see me coming, it ought to make you proud,' to borrow a line from Maya Angelou – phenomenal woman. And what you see is a woman so full, I'm overflowing with enough to share with everybody else. I am going to own the fullness without ego, without arrogance but with an amazing sense of gratitude." We've all seen her do it. I find it touching how after all these years, this phenomenal woman still says she works at being full. While abundance is the boundless nature of nature, we keep having to remind ourselves of that. It takes work to be an open channel for kindness, empathy and love, including tough love, even for the likes of Oprah.

Curiosity, an inalienable inexhaustible inquisitiveness, is another of our core gifts. We are the ones with the perennial questions. We take joy in investigating a subject to the bone, digging deeper, understanding better, knowing more… and a bit more still. We know no limits in our thirst to get to the bottom of this extraordinary human existence. In this hectic world with so much on offer, we never tire of learning more. We become the journalists who throw themselves heart and soul into the world news day after day, insatiable like the title of journalist and political commentator Megyn Kelly's book *Settle for More*.

Generosity is our middle name. In the throes of ongoing scarcity-thinking we might not have said so, but once we step out of that loop into our true nature, we will find how much we like to share. Sharing an experience heightens our awareness, deepens friendships, the bond we feel with people who were complete strangers a moment ago. If only we can relax and know that we give just by being ourselves when we are not even aware of giving. Generosity wants nothing in return, and will be rewarded a thousand-fold.

The will to live was what drove us to despair when no one came to feed or hold us. This will to live, to push on, to go further is part of our vivacity. With our broad interests, engagement and eagerness to know everybody as well as everything about everybody, we are naturally gregarious. We want to drink the last drop out of the cup of life, and are delighted to share our exploits with others. We love to meet new people, and have them be part of our lively crowd.

Talents honed

Ambition is one quality that springs from not knowing when enough is enough. "My attitude is never to be satisfied, never enough, never," pianist, jazz composer and bandleader Duke Ellington said. Grandson of a former slave, he wrote over a thousand musical pieces, and kept at it until the very last days of his life. Further and further, beyond what may satisfy others, more to do, to know, to understand, to experience – which official organization will ever let us know when enough is enough? There is no such board to give us a stamp of approval. We must become our own measuring stick and if we pay attention, we are well aware of how different we feel when the dread of not-enough is driving us or when we are thrust forward by our innate curiosity and will to make a difference.

Feeling that we cannot possibly ask for help, we develop an antenna for those who need help from us. Knowing how it feels to be left to our own devices, we compensate by kindling our diligence, becoming attentive friends, lovers and colleagues. We remember their birthdays, the day they get the results of a test. Never really knowing when is enough, we overload them with texts and messages so they really, really know we care about them.

Eloquence is another quality we cultivate. Many of us have a ready tongue; we know what we are on about and can convey it well. We are the teachers who year after year are able to bring the same subjects to life for a new generation of children. We are to be found in all professions where we can be the centre of attention as actors, authors, bloggers and vloggers, performers, politicians, presenters, motivational speakers, trainers, conductors or, if our language is music, the first violinist.

Never quite sure we've contributed enough, we are the ultimate volunteers as we are always willing to pitch in and lend a hand. Taking care of a friend's child after school, covering for an absent colleague or cooking for a sickly neighbour; we can always squeeze it into our busy schedule somehow. People wonder how we stretch time to fit everything in. Generally, we are hard workers. Somehow or other, we do what's needed. Soldiering on, we get a lot done. Our willingness to jump in is testimony to our innate good nature.

The paradox of needs

The childhood conclusion "There isn't enough, I am not enough" goes with a paradox of needing and denying our needs. Longing for attention, time and love, we don't want to ask for it, because if we ask for it, what we receive isn't real. The other must give it freely because they want to, but then again, if we don't ask, we are afraid we will get nothing at all. We love to give, but if we give to get we only exhaust ourselves, as what we get seems never to be in equal measure to what we give. In other words:

THE PARADOX
I would like someone to be there for me, but if I ask, it isn't real and if I don't ask, I most probably won't get it.

This quandary rears its head in all our relationships as we tend to complicate life with guessing games. As children, we may stubbornly keep at our homework that we don't understand because we don't want to ask our parents or older siblings for help – they have eyes, don't they? They can see we're in over our heads, can't they? Feeling like this, we may sit commiserating with ourselves while others think we're just working hard. Or don't think about us at all as they are engrossed in getting their own tasks finished.

At work, we may plough on rather than indicating to our boss or colleagues that we are overstretched. At home, we might despair that we are again the ones left with household chores while others go on their merry way. Whatever our inner whimpering is about isn't really the point – we want something from someone else. We aren't going to ask for anything, though. Instead, we send out subtle signals and start to watch whether these are being picked up. When the other person, completely unaware of our schemes, doesn't respond, we become more and more miserable. Inside, the whimpering grows in strength and conviction: "See – I always have to do everything on my own. No one ever helps out. No one sees all the tasks I take on. No one really appreciates me. They never have and never will. I am not going to ask for assistance, though; everyone can see what I need. They're just not forthcoming. No one ever is." Before we know it, we push on with a dour expression while our partner or colleague is completely oblivious to what it is we want from them. The whole scene unfolds on the vast stage in our minds.

Love is a great field of practice when we are caught in this paradox. In a love relationship, we must surrender emotionally to another. This is precisely what people who believe that the road to happiness leads through independence wish most to avoid. It may seem very reasonable these days not to want to marry but rather to live together. No one will blink an eye if life partners don't open a joint bank account; they each earn their own keep and they share expenses in the way they see fit. Yet, when we dig a bit deeper, not wanting to commit fully might, just might be a result of us not daring to depend on someone else again. If that is the case, the choice is not nearly as free as it may seem and examining the underlying childhood conclusion might be a good thing to do. Are we still being run by the fear that if push comes to shove we can't depend on someone we love? If this is the case, our relationship might benefit from tracking when we shy away from further intimacy as an adult on the basis of our perception as an infant.

The healing response

This childhood conclusion remains a tough one for me, especially when I have to wait my turn at a counter and the person in front of me is painfully slow – why are they only fishing their wallet out of their tote now when they could easily have done it while they were still queuing up? "Can't they see that I'm in a hurry?" hiss the inner thoughts that like to exaggerate my importance and want everyone to cater to me straight away, so I can get back to My Extremely Significant Activities.

Fortunately, these days I often have the presence of mind to apply the healing response to myself before I begin to sniff and to huff. I put my right hand on my left shoulder as if to cradle the hungry baby I once was. It is an unobtrusive gesture that nobody notices, and it allows me to calm my racing mind and start to enjoy the luxury of doing nothing for a few moments while I wait.

Simultaneously, I inwardly recite the mantra "There is enough, I have enough, I am enough." I recall times when I felt appreciated and loved, when I felt the flow of life carrying me rather than me making things happen by the sheer force of my dogged endurance. I remember my father's eyes as we exchanged our last words before he passed, and the love that flowed between us. I go to the sense of promise in spring, the feeling of expansion when seeing the sea, the abundance of products in the store I am in.

Physically, I move my jaw to relax it, and make a smile appear on my face. The smile I longed for as a child is a smile I can now give to myself. The appreciation, the adoration, the love – whatever I longed for when I was small, I can now give to myself; we can all give to ourselves, even when standing in a queue to pay for groceries.

Every moment we are alive is a miracle, never to come back again and quickly followed by another and another. The universe is one huge marvel in which planets hang together so that our lives are possible. From need and greed, a healing response makes me move to generosity and gratitude.

Apply lavishly, the instructions wrapped around an expensive sun cream I once bought said. Ah, my mean mind thought at the time, this is how you make sure you hoover up our money. It's a good advice, though: apply this healing response lavishly. Let us heap it on ourselves the moment devious not-enough doubts grab us by the throat. Let's replace this downward spiralling with thoughts that everyone in essence is enough, not too much, not too little, exactly enough. Let's look at each other with kind eyes – so many of us suffer from this delusion that we are the ones sadly falling short. Harking back to the very hungry caterpillar with a line from Rabindranath Tagore, "The butterfly counts not months but moments, and has time enough."

Turning this childhood conclusion

How would we be different if we could ask for what we needed and gracefully receive it? Can we even imagine life without the tension we feel in a queue, a waiting room or a traffic jam? Have we had enough of thoughts whispering that we just aren't adequate and up to the mark, or that it's our turn to get some attention, for once? Turning the persistent thoughts stemming from this babyhood conviction can pull the plug on the restricted awareness that sees only shortage, shortfall and scarcity. This frame sets out the five steps.

STEP 1: recognize the thought pattern

We can prick up our ears when we hear ourselves repeating the words "not enough", either out loud or internally. The first step is merely beginning to notice those "not enough" thoughts – that there isn't enough, or that we are not enough – and realizing that they spring from a conclusion we drew when we were tiny.

STEP 2: shift the focus

We consciously ground ourselves in this moment, in who we have grown into. As who we have become, we may take the needy child that we were into our arms, as it were, and cherish it as one of life's many miracles. This phenomenal manifestation of life itself – how could it possibly not be enough?

STEP 3: thank ourselves

The scarcity thought pattern is rooted in babyhood, when for one reason or another we got an impression of lack and deficiency. Wanting to be fed more or held longer, waiting in mortal fear that nobody would come, we transformed the absence of outer attention into a personal deficiency. We can now thank the part of us that, with the perspective of a baby, saw this as the only possible explanation.

STEP 4: invite the dread from back then

As the adult, we can face up to the consternation from so long ago. We will again feel the terrible terror we felt as a baby, the despair that we had been abandoned to our fate. If we can keep this up for a few minutes, we will find that the fear fades away by itself, and with it the thoughts that we are not enough.

STEP 5: live our life, no holds barred

Enough is as good as a feast – we can create unending enjoyment in life. We don't need anything or anyone else for that. We are enough as we are, and have plenty to share for others. From a chronic sense of scarcity, we move to gratitude as the ground of our existence.

The first three steps

Just as with the previous childhood conclusion, we can do the first three steps whenever we need to and wherever we are. The "not-enough" feeling can stick to absolutely anything, and can creep up on us seemingly out of the blue. No one else needs notice a thing as we focus on who we are now and unmask and thank the reiterating thoughts that we are not or have not enough.

STEP 1: recognize the thought pattern

Thoughts come and go like birds in the sky. If we feed them, birds will flock to us in great numbers. When we just watch them, they pay us no attention and go their own way. The same goes for our thoughts.

In this first step, we are not going to feed insufficiency thoughts, but just watch them and check the facts: do we truly not have enough money, time, clothes or brain cells? Or are we stuck in the rut of an old pattern that keeps deluding us that there is not enough, that we are not enough?

We can also listen to the inner tone of voice. Does it sound like moaning and whining? If so, we can be almost certain that these thoughts are being produced by this childhood conclusion. The little words "always" and "never" may also alert us, as do overpowering feelings of impatience. Sometimes instead of overt thoughts, we find a bad feeling stealing over us, out of all proportion to what is actually happening. This, too, is the young childhood conclusion making itself known.

STEP 2: shift the focus

We are no longer that hungry baby whose life depended on the next feed. We have survived our early days, have learned a lot and been around the block a few times. We are now plugging the hole that we feel inside, that can be filled by nothing except our own self-esteem. We can look back on our lives from the perspective of who we have become. Our context is much bigger than it was then. Feeling who we are now, complete with all those difficult feelings of insecurity, through all those times when we believed that everyone knew better or could do better than us, we have grown into the person we are now. Just like everybody else, we are someone with unique gifts. We are neither too much nor too little. While we are growing through experience each and every day, we are enough, exactly enough. Now there's a thought worth believing.

STEP 3: thank ourselves

You may be thinking at this point: "Curiouser and curiouser! Do I even have to *thank* that awful feeling?" Well, I don't know what else you have tried in your life, but my experience is that thanking works faster and more effectively than anything else. When we drew this childhood conclusion, we had the perspective of a child a few hours, days or weeks old. Our parents did what they could – they are not to blame. Maybe we had carers who weren't really there for us, but even so, it is pointless to make reproaches.

As infants, we projected the outer feeling of deficiency inwards. We started feeling that we ourselves were lacking, flawed, unsatisfactory. That thought has produced all kinds of feelings of insecurity, possibly even fear of failure. That feeling of "not enough" is also the source of our ambition. We don't know enough, so we must learn more. We don't earn enough, so we must climb higher. That drive has contributed to who we are in all kinds of ways. So, thanking is in order, saying something like: "I really value that I have become who I am. Thank you for having brought me so far."

Perhaps we will spontaneously begin to sigh – as if a heavy burden has been lifted from our shoulders. At last this part of us that worked overtime to remind us that there wasn't enough and that we always had to go higher, further, faster may now take a well-deserved break.

A common theme

Luis has announced that he is resigning from the school board because he finds he is not playing his role adequately. To his great discomfort, his fellow board members don't agree to his stepping down. "Don't worry," they say, "we all felt disoriented at the beginning. The jargon and abbreviations, the long history with some teachers, it takes a bit of time to get the hang of it. Please, if there's something you don't know, just ask. We've been working together for so long – it's really good for us to have to describe how things work around here."

It has never occurred to Luis that other people might feel as unskillful as he does. He feels shy now he has laid himself open, but as he looks around, he sees only friendly faces. He realizes that he has fallen into his own "not enough" trap. He shifts his focus back to the man he has become, the person his colleagues on the board reflect to him. Silently he thanks the part of him that has always prompted him to do his best and has shepherded him into who he is.

The questions he starts to ask lead to interesting discussions and new solutions. It slowly begins to dawn on Luis that he is a capable, likeable man. He needs less affirmation from the people around him. He is no less willing than before to take on tasks, but he starts to see when he jumps in to get recognition and appreciation, and when he volunteers just because he enjoys helping out.

"I'm no longer giving from a void," he comments. "Now I simply give what I have to contribute. Without ulterior motives. I was always scared to be a disappointment to others. That's why I was forever either knocking myself down or proving myself. Thanks to my colleagues on this board, I have come to see that we are a team, and that it doesn't all depend on me. It sounds crazy, but I really thought that. Now that I have stilled these thoughts that take me down, it's as if I have stepped out of the woods onto a wide ocean beach."

Fully turning this childhood conclusion

The portal to happiness is shaped by what we most want to avoid. As a baby we felt terrified, miserable, neglected, abandoned, disappointed. We had no words in those days, but we felt mortally afraid: if we weren't fed soon, it was game over. We still get that feeling regularly. Every time we don't feel adequate, when we are made to wait, when we have overcommitted ourselves, that babyhood feeling is reproduced.

Turning the childhood conclusion fully will help. Revisiting the first three steps, we begin by noticing thoughts that would have us believe there is not enough and we are not enough. Realizing we are no longer a vulnerable baby but a valued adult, we express gratitude for how this early-life conviction has set us on our particular path. We might want to find somewhere quiet to sit or lie down, making sure we are warm enough and can relax. As who we are now, we will revisit a recent situation where we felt that there was not enough time or attention for us, or that we were not good enough.

STEP 4: invite the fear from back then

This step is an invitation to return to a situation in which thoughts kept telling us that we were falling short or an occasion of being awash with feelings that there wasn't enough time or attention for us. This is not about how we solved the situation, but about staying in the feeling that we never get enough attention, that our turn never comes, that we probably aren't going to measure up.

We might have to practise a bit in order to be able to reproduce that feeling on command. If this is the case, allow the feeling that we might not even be good enough to complete this exercise to expand. Perhaps we unconsciously pinch our lips together, let the shoulders hang or feel pain in the chest. It might help to exaggerate these bodily expressions. Can we feel that basic fear again now as we recall how it is to feel there simply is not enough for us and of us?

The intention is not to get stuck in this fear. The point is to let go of the awful feeling that often overcomes us, by gently letting that old agony back in, feeling it fully knowing that we are about to let it go. With some practice, we can let the feeling of deficiency and scarcity grow until the throat contracts, the strength leaks from the arms, our heart pounds – however the dejection manifests in your body. The trick is just to feel what we feel without wanting to change or direct anything.

At a first attempt it might not prove easy to contact the feeling and magnify it to get the full healing effect. Many of us are used to talking about feelings of inadequacy, but not to actually feeling them. Just see how far you get. Every time is good enough. If we manage to let the fear come up, then let the feeling of deficiency and inadequacy flow. If we allow it to take us over while we are centred in our adult self, it will grow and… dissolve. This process won't last more than a few minutes. If it lasts any longer, we have probably given way to the sorrow and since this is about coming out of grief, the remedy is to shift the focus back to who we are now. Also, we don't want to overwork this process out of fear of not having done enough or not having gone deep enough.

Grounded in the adult self, we can be like a bowl that holds the old fear and pain but which itself is not affected by it. Once we have dared to feel our childhood terror fully, it evaporates and old thoughts will gradually be replaced by new ones: "I am enough; exactly enough. What I don't know, I shall learn, but as a person, I am enough. I am as pleasant as I can be at this moment, as attractive as I am, as funny as I can be. And that is enough. Not too much, not too little, exactly enough."

STEP 5: live our life, no holds barred

Realizing that I am just right as I am at this moment still moves me. I sometimes hear a small voice in me piping up: "Can it really be true?" The answer is: yes! I have as much ambition and drive as ever but, now that I find myself adequate, my fuel comes from another source. Where I used to think that I had to prove I was enough, and did things to get something back in the way of appreciation or praise or even just being seen, these days I act from an inner drive. I am rewarded by the act itself, not by what it might bring me.

We folk with this childhood conclusion are curious. We always want to know and see more, and that brings its own satisfactions. We can offer the world the qualities that we have developed thanks to this childhood conclusion. We are generous givers of time and energy. It cannot be repeated often enough (pun intended): we know enough, we are capable of enough, we are enough.

A positive present

As soon as a "not enough" thought arises, as soon as we feel we are being ignored or that we are a disappointment, we can do ourselves a big favour by giving ourselves the healing response. We can combine this with the quick method of the first three steps of turning habitual childhood conclusion thoughts. Treating ourselves to all five steps every so often will help us gain more distance from feelings of disappointment and deficiency. A time will come when we will notice our thoughts naturally going along these lines:

POSTIVE SELF-TALK
There is enough.
There is enough time, enough attention, enough friendship.
There is enough of all the truly important things in life.
I am enough.
I am neither too much, nor too little, but just right.
I am as I am, and that is enough.
I am likeable/attentive/loveable/good-looking/smart enough.
If ever I am not, I learn my lesson and move on.
I am learning to ask for what I want and what I need.
I don't have to go it alone.
I don't need to attract all the attention.
I no longer give in order to get.
I enjoy giving.
I create sufficiency in life.
I am enough.

Once we feel enough, our sense of self-worth is no longer dependent on recognition from outside ourselves. The mind-boggling thing is that, once we feel "enough", we will soon find we have more time. All that time we used to spend on silently bemoaning what a disappointment we were, or wondering what we could expect from someone else who would surely let us down again – all that time is now ours. We must all learn to become who we are in this life. We are all just right.

Pause to reflect

On the difference between reflection and obsessing,
overreacting and underreacting, the gift of the healing
response and how the next three childhood conclusions
build on the first two.

Feeling our infant fears in order to turn them into a positive present is
hard work. Let's take a short break and consider the difference between
thoughts that arise from childhood conclusions and adult reflection. Certainly not every thought of needing to leave and go elsewhere stems from the first
childhood conclusion. When we're in a fashionable restaurant where we can't
hear our companion even though they're speaking at the top of their voice, we
might want to go elsewhere. No fuss – we'll be back when we prefer mood or
food over a conversation or relaxation.

Nor will every moment we feel we don't have enough time or aren't on
top of things enough arise from the second childhood conclusion. Contemplating how a presentation went while on the way home is a valuable
adult skill. When we're honestly evaluating what went well and what could
have been better, we may conclude that on points we could have come more
prepared. This type of mature self-assessment is a very different activity from
when our thoughts are in childhood conclusion-rehashing mode, and our
incessant self-talk has us reliving scares from the past while projecting them
into the present.

In her insightful book *Reclaiming Your Life*, psychotherapist Jean Jenson
gives a good pointer on how to make that distinction. She describes how
overreacting and underreacting both point to having returned to a childhood
state of consciousness. "Whenever we under- or overreact to something, the

mind has shifted from the adult state of consciousness to that of childhood, and we temporarily experience the world from the dependent position of a child," she writes. "Either we are flooded with feelings that are out of proportion to the present reality, or we shut down emotionally, automatically defending ourselves from a potential onslaught. In the latter situation, we are not even aware that feelings are present, waiting to be felt."

Applying Jenson's observation to the first two childhood conclusions helps greatly in discerning when we have shifted from adult to child consciousness. Overreacting in situations that trigger the first conclusion that we are not welcome and don't truly belong will express itself in hyperactivity, wanting to be everywhere at the same time and not here at all. Underreacting, we leave; we fly away to other realms and absent ourselves from this one. Underreacting from the second childhood conclusion that there is not enough and we are not enough will show up in the denial that we need anything from anyone at all. We will not even be able to feel our needs, and wonder what people who have them are on about. Overreaction will make us be impatient, assertive and vocal, claiming attention and wanting – no, demanding the floor.

Always one or two

Theory has it that everyone jumps to one or both of the first two childhood conclusions. Everyone. That means that at least half of us are haunted by the belief that we shouldn't be here, and don't live fully in our bodies. It also means that those who have drawn the first conclusion may also have jumped to the second. This leads to the staggering realization that more than half of us struggle with self-talk insisting there is not enough and we are not enough.

When I first heard this thesis I found it, frankly, hard to believe. Then, when I considered the people who came to see me in my private practice, I had to concede it was true. Granted, they all came with a life question so they may not be representative. Yet I dare you to look around your circle of friends, name the gifts you see they have even if they aren't bringing them out in full force yet, and begin a conversation on the kind of self-talk they engage in. You will probably be as surprised as I was to learn that most of us just don't feel up to snuff. We try to hide our perceived incompetence but when someone starts a conversation on the topic, many in the circle will confess to beating themselves up regularly for "just not having what it takes".

Rewiring for happiness

Bringing joy to others and drawing out the best in them is the surest way to personal happiness. Just imagine for a moment how much good we could do merely by instilling in ourselves a healing response of being welcome and being enough before going out the door. This would have us walking around consciously fostering a sense of welcome and sufficiency. Conveying these messages energetically, with our eyes and our words, could be our good deed for the day.

A bonus of emanating belonging and enoughness is the fantastic feeling it generates in ourselves. As Bruce Lipton shows in *The Biology of Belief*, our cells' operations are primarily moulded by interaction with the environment, not by genetic code. If we walk around consciously choosing to think uplifting thoughts, we will see our environment as benign, maybe even beautiful. Research has confirmed that our brain cells translate the mind's subjective perceptions into chemical profiles that are released in the blood and determine how we feel. "That explains why my health and energy soared," Lipton writes, "after I jettisoned my old 'depressed, fatalistic' view of the world." He cites several studies that show that a positive mindset can even undo some of the effects of ageing; so while we are using our healing response as a blessing for others, we might even be reversing the ageing process of our cells more effectively than the most expensive moisturizer money can buy.

"Experience molds our brain," confirm Daniel Siegel and Tina Payne Bryson in *The Whole-Brain Child*. "Even into old age, our experiences actually change the physical structure of the brain. This is incredibly exciting news. It means that we aren't held captive by the way our brain works at this moment – we can actually rewire it so that we can be healthier and happier."

On to the next three

More gifts are waiting to be uncovered, so let's prepare for further transformation of the pejorative into the positive. We draw the next three childhood conclusions somewhat later in our young lives. Our brains have already downloaded incredible amounts of information that allow us to talk, to be self-aware and conscious of the role we play within the constellation of the family.

We still don't venture out very far yet and so it is natural for us to assume that how things go in our household is how things go everywhere.

Being children, we even now operate from a small frame of reference. We're continuing to develop our inner world by observing the little circle of people around us. We faithfully record what is being said and done in our immediate surroundings without making distinctions between opinion and fact. It's all information to us, as we ourselves are in the process of being rapidly formed. If our immediate family don't like something we do, we are quick to assume they don't like *us*. That hits home hard. In an involuntary attempt to be loved and cherished again, we respond by hiding, dominating or adapting. These three strategies are at the core of the next three conclusions that we draw: hiding our innate creativity, dominating in order to remain in control and adapting to fit in.

The three later childhood conclusions superimpose themselves on the first two. Then, of course, the thoughts that are generated by each of the childhood conclusions start to mutually reinforce one another. Thus it can happen that our proclivity towards moving out of our body because of feeling unwelcome is strengthened by the experience of people violating our boundaries, which leads to the third childhood conclusion. The early conclusion that we are not enough can come back to haunt us in full force when, on top of that, we experience rejection of our love by one of our parents; we will see that this is the cause of the fourth childhood conclusion that we had better stay in control. The fifth childhood conclusion tells us we need to behave properly, but when are we proper enough, is what the second childhood conclusion wants to know.

A few notes can build a catchy tune and the existence of songs galore is tribute to the endless creative expression we can achieve with the same limited means. Similarly, with the feelings and thoughts arising from all five childhood conclusions we each construct a unique life path of recovering and consciously cultivating the gifts we bring.

3

Willing to create

CHILDHOOD CONCLUSION
"What do I know – have it your way."

NEGATIVE SELF-TALK
"Who am I to talk? People will overstep my boundaries left and right. Nothing I can do about it but show a funny face and make sure I keep my fuming anger down."

CORE GIFTS
creativity, compassion, playfulness, joy

A child hums happily while drawing a cat. She is completely consumed by the fantasy world she still partially lives in, so the drawing comes to life and together with the cat the child has whole adventures in a world all their own. The mother happens by and comments: "What a funny little fox you have drawn there."

"It is a cat," mumbles the girl, still fully concentrated on her game.

"No, darling," the mother corrects, "the snout is too pointed and look at its tail. No, you drew a beautiful little fox here. How sweet to have made this for me."

The child is astounded. For her mummy? It is a cat and it is her cat that she is having all kinds of adventures with.

"Here, give it to me and I will hang it on the fridge," the mother continues happily, "so we can all enjoy it."

The mother leaves the child behind in a state of confusion. One moment she was playing with the cat she had drawn, the next instant the cat was objected to and the drawing confiscated. The child cannot comprehend how this could have happened so quickly. She finds herself in two minds. She would love to continue playing with her new friend the cat, but doesn't want to go and take the drawing down from the fridge as she doesn't want to disappoint or contradict her mother. The resolution to this predicament is that the child makes up a new imaginary cat to play with. To make sure she can keep it to herself, she doesn't draw it this time.

When the father sees the drawing and the mother tells him it is a fox, he smiles at his wunderkind. What can the child do? If she tells him she drew a cat, he will get confused and then Mummy will argue that it is a fox anyway. If she doesn't protest about the wrong impression her father now has, the child feels, it is dishonest for her to be praised for having drawn a fox. "It was a cat," she mutters in a disempowered voice, too quiet to be heard. Like any other child, she would love to please her parents, make them proud, but she also feels angry with the mother for taking the cat away. She feels like a pawn with her mother who took her drawing from her and she feels like a cheat with her father, as she can't possibly tell him the whole story of what happened earlier on. Also she has to hide her sadness at losing her fictional playmate from both parents.

The girl feels bewildered. She decides to "bury" the cat. Deep within. Safety, is the inescapable conclusion, is in not showing what lives inside us and in swallowing our resentment about what is taken from us. As a consequence of such and other instances in which our privacy is invaded, we start to hide our natural creativity and our life force. We show the world a happy face so no one will ask for what we are keeping secret. We cultivate a sense of humour as a way to direct the attention away from the vault we are protecting. We bury our confusion, with our resentment and anger, so deep within that a state of overwhelm becomes our habitat.

Creativity stunted

This conclusion "What do I know – have it your way" may also arise at the time of potty-training. Under the expectant gaze of one or both parents, as a child we have to produce bodily waste that cannot always be planned for.

Crowing with pleasure, the boy pees all over the place although he was supposed to poo neatly in the pot. "That was not what we agreed," the parents say with a clear sigh of disappointment. "What we agreed? How can this be something to agree upon?" the child wonders. "What comes is what comes. This is how it has always been and it has never been an issue before."

The boy doesn't understand what has changed all of a sudden. He has been pooing when not on the pot for so long, and then it turns out this is no longer desirable. How bewildering – he has produced what his parents asked for, but something must inexplicably have gone awry. With a growing sense of despair the child tries to fulfil his parents' wishes. He is perplexed as to what exactly is expected, uncomprehendingly does the wrong thing and feels deeply ashamed of not managing to deliver on demand. Keeping whatever he needs to do inside as long as possible in an attempt to not goof up again has the inevitable consequence – that things come out involuntarily at undesirable moments, which makes his parents throw their hands in the air and sigh that they doubt if this child will ever learn.

It goes without saying that the process of becoming potty-trained doesn't have every child jumping to this childhood conclusion. It can, however, be a time of confusion and public humiliation, with not only parents but perhaps older children also chiming in about what you ought and ought not to produce at the apparent right time. In order not to suffer such public humiliation again, we'd rather never produce anything any more, but life doesn't work that way. Just like everybody else, we will need to make our contribution.

When the childhood conclusion of not having any power over our life gets the better of us, it makes us procrastinate, postpone and agonize. This childhood conclusion is about autonomy, about us feeling okay exploring the world on our own and exposing ourselves as we're doing so.

Boundaries violated

The childhood conclusion that it is better to keep the products of our creativity inside is also drawn by people whose boundaries have been violated when they were small. Very often these invasive acts were performed by people they know, grown-ups they trust. Little boys are being groped by the neighbour who is such good friends with their parents. What does the child do? What can he do? Girls keep silent about the nights their father comes to caress them in a manner they don't like. Their mother looks the other way. What should the girl do?

If the grown-ups pretend nothing is the matter, the child often complies while knowing deep down that something totally wrong is going on. Instead of blaming the adults, as a child we often blame ourselves; we feel that we have somehow provoked these awful acts that we are unable to prevent from happening again and again. When we say "no" to the unwanted expressions of "love", we are not listened to. We are seduced into cooperation or overruled by mere force. When we don't put up a fight against what we don't want, we point the arrow inwards and despise our own weakness. We feel gullible, duped and completely without power. Burdened by guilt and shame, we dare not divulge our secret. The only way to endure our painful situation seems to be to swallow the anxiety, humiliation and fear we feel, and try to protect our innermost core so we will somehow remain pure where it matters most. Out of what happens we draw the conclusion that we have no say over our own life at all and it is better to keep silent so at least no one knows our horrible secret.

The World Health Organization acknowledges child maltreatment as a global problem with serious lifelong consequences. They define child maltreatment as abuse and neglect that happens to children under eighteen years of age, and include all types of physical and/or emotional ill-treatment, sexual abuse, neglect, negligence and commercial or other exploitation, which results in actual or potential harm to the child's health, survival, development or dignity in the context of a relationship of responsibility, trust or power.

The horrid fact is that a quarter of all the adults report having been physically abused as children; and one in five women and one in 13 men report having been sexually abused as a child. Additionally, many children are subject to emotional abuse, which is sometimes referred to as psychological abuse, and to neglect. The WHO state that consequences of child maltreatment include impaired lifelong physical and mental health. As adults, the organization says, maltreated children are at increased risk for behavioural, physical and mental health problems such as perpetrating or being a victim of violence, depression, smoking, obesity, high-risk sexual adventuring, unintended pregnancy and alcohol and drug misuse.

Victim – survivor – thriver

As a well-respected and beloved member of the Findhorn Foundation Community in northern Scotland, Lesley Quilty was asked to give a TEDx Talk the first time such an event was organized there in 2015. Quilty paints the picture of her family breaking down after her father suddenly dropped dead of a heart attack. She goes on to talk openly of how a kind man offered her as a needy 11-year-old the love and the holding she longed for; but it came in the form of a sexually abusive relationship.

It is very silent in the Universal Hall as she speaks. If the horrifying statistics are true, many of those present must have experienced some form of abuse in their lives, or loved someone who has. As an accomplished personal coach and a clown, Quilty acknowledges that her opening up what most of us prefer to keep hidden might provoke feelings of rage, terror, shame or numbness. She invites the audience to see her as living proof that the inner voice that says we will never get over it might not be right. "We might get over it," Quilty says. "I am on a continuous journey from being a victim to being a survivor to being a thriver. I may never reach the final destination, but I am on the road." She points the virtual road signs out with her hands: victim – survivor – thriver.

Self-fulfilling fear

With his beaming round face, Harry looks much younger than his age. He is now head of the human resources department of the firm he joined two decades ago, and his management style is still to have time for everyone, making no distinction between the CEO and the receptionist. However, the request to revise a policy on equal opportunity has now been on his desk for a while already.

"I just need to check a few more things," he has been telling himself every Friday. "I will get around to it next week." The deadline for delivery long past, the policy begins to be a source of shame for himself and the butt of jokes among his colleagues. Harry cringes when the policy paper comes up on the agenda in a meeting, he suffers under the pressure from his staff, he agonizes over his own sense of failure. Even then, he is unable to bring himself to share what he has got written with his colleagues out of fear that they might throw it back on his desk, laughing. Like a horse refusing to jump a fence, he doesn't move. Just won't do it.

He has had this happen to him before but it seems to get worse. He is only nominally a manager, his thoughts tell him over and over again; in truth his colleagues and bosses determine his agenda. He doesn't let on, but secretly he rages against his superiors, who have an easy life with a dutiful donkey like himself running the show. He looks up to people who have the reins of their lives firmly in their own hands, but when he stops to think about it, even people high up in positions of power seem to be run by the news of the day.

Maybe no one has a life of their own, is how he consoles himself. On the way home he stops to fill up his tank and comes out with three Mars bars and a large ice-cream. His increasing weight is another stigma as it displays his lack of self-control for all the world to see, and to ridicule him. He strengthens his intention to finalize the wretched policy next week, and to begin to eat less tomorrow. In his heart, he knows he will do neither. "What for heaven's sake is the matter with me?" he thinks, squirming.

This is where insight into the feelings and thoughts of shame and needing to avoid public humiliation that arise from this childhood conclusion come in. When the refusal to deliver what is required is this strong, we may want to examine the underlying thought patterns that keep us paralyzed – and be forgiving, as they arise from a period in our lives when our boundaries were violated, when our "no" was not respected and we felt there was no choice but to go along with the adults' wishes. We swallowed our anger as we didn't dare put the love of our parents or other authority figures at risk – and at the same time we got confused by apparently having no power to stop the invasive or humiliating action. We allowed the awful experience to happen, kept a brave face outwardly and inwardly retreated to a place of hiding deep within ourselves. "Okay then – what do I know, have it your way and I will stick it out and keep quiet" is the tone of the tumbling mix of feelings and thoughts we had at the time, even if we were too young to describe the conundrum we found ourselves in against our will.

Growing up with this childhood conclusion

"The first thing to understand," psychotherapist Jean Jenson writes about the way children cope with abusive experiences, "is that there are experiences that are too painful for a child to feel. There are also certain realities, certain truths about our parents and our families, that are too painful for children to know about." She describes how children who are powerless to change these situations come to rely on the self-protective defences of repression and denial. In repression we force the memory of the dreadful event into the unconscious mind. In denial we refuse to acknowledge the truth before us. Underreacting in the case of these childhood experiences comes in the form of emotional shutdown and going numb. This strategy also makes us play dumb when we are afraid that what we say might be wrong. Overreaction is when we respond to the disempowerment of others overly emotionally, as the response is not really to their current predicament but to horrible experiences in our own past.

In day-to-day life, as children who are clobbered by thoughts of needing to keep our life force down and our creative expression hidden we often get on people's nerves. We put their patience to the test with our endless dithering and immobilizing inability to make a choice. We try desperately to gauge what the people around us want in order to have a point of reference, but that is a complicated and time-consuming process that has us hovering and hesitating over small decisions for ages. "Will the choice be made today?" fathers, mothers, friends and teachers wonder. "Get on with it!"

As adolescents, we are dubbed passive-aggressive as we say "yes" and do "no". It is not that we aren't utterly willing to do as we promised; it's just that we need time to figure out how to do a job in order to get it right, while not being sure what right actually looks like. We keep others waiting. They start wondering if they might take the task on themselves – be it as trivial as clearing the table, watering the plants or feeding the fish – so at least they know it is done. When out of exasperation they complete what was ours to do, we feel robbed yet again of an opportunity to express ourselves in our very own way.

Dragging our feet, we create a confusion in the outside world that mirrors the inner labyrinth we have built on the basis of this childhood conclusion. Having piled anger upon anger, frustration upon frustration while keeping our creative impulses in check, we are like a thousand-drawer treasure trove without an index of where to find what. Part of our endless stalling and procrastinating on making choices is that we have no clue where to go to look for our desires and needs beneath the many layers of stacked resentment.

We might get into the habit of keeping mum as we can't get it wrong if we don't say anything. We downplay our grief and loneliness: "Chin up. Surely people are living through circumstances much worse than me." Such whitewashing feeds into the sense of humour we develop to distract the attention from ourselves and thus enhance our invisibility. Our quips are often loaded with self-mockery. "Ah, that's me again, the clumsy clown who trips over a banana peel," we say when we knock over a cup of coffee. We laugh our sense of public humiliation away.

Within the family, we are the ones who good-humouredly defuse the tension in the air. With our cakes, quiches and casseroles we are considered sweethearts. We are indeed, as in all kinds of ways we allow other people to come first. "All right with me," is our standard reply when a sibling switches the channel while we were watching our favourite series. "No sweat," we mutter when we are the last to be chosen for the team in the sports class. Shrugging our shoulders, we show a happy face while inside we wage a war.

This rage, however, we dare not show; frankly, we don't see how we could. We build a reservoir of resentment and anger that grows every time we don't stand up to what we don't wish to have happen to us. The more wrath we store, the greater the fluster and the conviction that we ourselves are to blame. It is not right to hate one's parents, one's siblings, one's bosses and colleagues, all figures of authority, people in politics and everyone who is thin; one is not supposed to feel that way. What happened to us as a child was not supposed to happen either but everyone kept quiet about that, and so we do what we can to keep mum, too. Jenson points out that the hurt in these children is greatly underestimated, even among those with enough understanding to recognize themselves as "adult children".

Overeat to be invisible

With a sigh, by demonstratively heaving our body out of a chair or by a pained sideways glance we may give others the uncanny feeling that they've done something wrong. When family or friends ask if anything is the matter, we will shake our head and say nothing is wrong – why would it be? We've been keeping our secret for too long to divulge it now. We wouldn't know where to start anyway in our confused inner inferno.

For many, one way to keep rage down, our sense of impotence numbed and creativity hidden is through eating. Every time we haven't kept our boundaries intact, every time we feel the anger rise or we are overwhelmed and feel unable to cope, we put something in our mouth. We quell the sense of failure with fatty snacks full of empty calories. We comfort ourselves with sweets that slow us down. We eat more, say less, grow our bodies bigger and keep smiling while we try to become invisible.

Sometimes, however, all of a sudden we can take it no more and for a seemingly nonsensical reason we explode. Like a volcano spewing lava, we throw out years of blazing frustration and infernal indignation. Friends and foes alike are taken by surprise, as they are used to us being in good spirits. We might stomp off, slamming the door in their face, to comfort ourselves with a soda and a snack, a sitcom.

Invariably after our show of belligerence we will be hit by fits of shame and blame. The others made us blow up. We of all people don't want to jeopardize the harmony as far as it exists. The perplexed reasoning has us back to laying the blame on our own shoulders. "Now look what you've done," we chide ourselves, resolving never to be brought to the disgraceful point of exploding again. As a result, we screw the lid on ever tighter. Withdrawing further and further into ourselves while eating away the last remnants of our self-respect, we may end up down in the depths of depression.

Negative self-talk

When childhood conclusion thoughts overwhelm us, we feel scared, frustrated, angry and sad all at the same time. We are afraid to be used as a doormat once more. We feel frustrated because we are not clear on what we want and seem unable to make even the simplest of choices. We try to please others and keep out of harm's way, but we still land ourselves in awkward situations, as pleasing everyone turns out to be an impossible task. We show a happy face to the world outside while the despair and anger bubble quite close to the surface, and we're terrified of letting off steam. While we attempt to remain invisible, the body expands without us seeming to be able to do anything about it.

What *can* we do anything about? When this deep sense of being powerless grabs us, we shrug and sigh, and push ourselves through the day as best we can. We plod on, hoping for better times ahead. The inner tape keeps running with self-diminishing thoughts like these:

NEGATIVE SELF-TALK

Whoever is in charge of my life, it isn't me.
When I give in to other people, at least they're happy.
What else can I do?
If I want something, I bet it's not allowed.
When I say something, it is generally misunderstood.
I had better keep my mouth shut.
I will keep smiling so I seem full of good cheer.
They don't listen to me anyway.
I should not let on what I feel.

I'm better off hiding my feelings.
I am furious but I must keep my rage inside.
I hate them, but I act as if nothing is wrong.
I can't resist them – can I?
I'd better play the fool, or I will explode.
I guess it is my fate to give in all the time.
I should just do what others think is good for me.
But it is so frustrating not to be able to go my own way.
If I only knew what my own way was.
I feel lost.
I resent all of them.
I hate them, I hate my life, I hate being me.
I want to be free of everyone and their stupid wishes.
I have to hide myself, make myself invisible.
Let me grab something to eat – that always helps.
When I eat, I feel good.
Or do I truly know how I feel?
I am not sure.
I can't help it, can I?

The habit of swallowing resistance and resentment and going along with what seems to be wanted from us is strong. "This is just how it is," we think when we are weighed down by this childhood conclusion that perpetuates a sense of victimhood. It seems impossible to alter our lives and the situations, big and small, we don't wish to be in. We will surely not be listened to… so we take another bite of food and scold ourselves once more for being weaklings who just let things slide.

We may come to a point of being fed up with the struggle and the victimhood, which is a good place to be in. This will make us go and rummage in the thousand-drawer treasure trove to find our original creative state of being.

Core gifts

Like everyone else, we were born with a wealth of talents and gifts. We have locked them away to keep them safe and untainted by what transpired when we were young. Once we start to turn this childhood conclusion, these gifts will help us take control of our own lives.

Creativity is the tool of the ongoing process of creation. Our natural creative impulse was so precious to us as children that when it was misunderstood, taken or violated we hid it deep within, and there it still is, unharmed, untouched, unspoilt. When step by small step we lay down the burden of self-recrimination, we will notice how our natural creativity starts to flow again. At work, in the kitchen, with friends, in the way we make connections between people who are happy to meet but would not have got together without us. When we no longer give others authority over our lives, we can begin to follow the threads of our creative impulses and weave our very own tapestry.

It might have been empathy that got us into trouble. His Holiness the Dalai Lama frequently states that the surest path to true happiness lies in being intimately concerned with the welfare of others. Together with love, sympathetic joy and equanimity, compassion is one of the four core qualities cultivated by those on the path of the Buddha like him. If empathy has us imagine how it would feel to be in someone else's shoes, compassion has us act on this awareness. Familiar with being treated as a doormat, we have compassion in spades. With this quality, we tend to find work in the social sector, in healthcare, the service industry and other jobs where attention for the other is central. We are able to take the sting out of sticky situations, precisely because everyone senses our deep respect for all involved. When shown gratitude for our caring efforts, we may begin by not waving it away. We may use the appreciation of others to acknowledge that the tender flame of wanting to make other people happy, which got us into trouble when young, still burns brightly in us.

We may look younger than we are because we tend to remain young at heart. Youthful and playful. As we come out of hiding, our playfulness will be able to flourish and bloom. We have an innate innocence, a way of taking things lightly however heavy they are, a natural sense that if we keep moving, keep the ball in the game, we will just be able to have fun. The game itself is the goal; we don't need to make one up. Playing includes fantasy and imagination, evokes merriment and laughter – and keeps us young.

All we ever really wanted was to share our joy as we feel it welling up in us. We can take pleasure in a daisy growing, the smile of an old friend, the slow dance of the waves on the ocean. Creation cannot help but create and there is boundless joy in all the shapes and forms that emerge, ever new and fresh as a spring breeze. Joy needs no reason or rhyme. It just is and it flows and spreads wherever it goes. *We* spread it wherever we go.

Talents honed

"Warm-hearted" is one of the traits people will attribute to us. They know they can always knock on our door for comfort and care. We will brew them tea, make them soup, have apple pie baking in the oven. We are the colleagues who will bring cake to a difficult meeting in order to sweeten the mood. We are the coach of the youth team with a kind word for each child. The more we are in touch with our innate creativity, the more we can be the intermediaries who can connect parties in such a way that everyone leaves happy with the results achieved.

Laughter is great medicine, and we have plenty of it. So far jocularity has been a means of directing attention away from us. This good humour will remain one of our great gifts when we stop making ourselves the butt of our jokes. Being silly, making people laugh and have a good time will stay part of why people like to be around us.

We have been in the role of victim long enough to know what it feels like to be disempowered, disenfranchised, dismissed. The course of our life has served to heighten our innate sense of justice. We may long have felt overwhelmed by all the sorrow in the world, but as we step out of self-recrimination we will step into empowered action, even if it is small. We do what we can, and we are in this together.

The disempowering paradox

The basis of every childhood conclusion is a paradox, one of life's inevitable riddles. Within those of us who feel slow, stuck and confused on a regular basis, who tend to make promises that we already know we are not going to fulfil, who set boundaries that we allow others to violate, who find it hard to say "no" even to what is harmful for ourselves, who suffer from self-revulsion, who knowingly let things slide and go wrong, and who keep resentment and rage buried by a copious intake of food, the underlying paradox might sound something like this:

THE PARADOX

When I stand up for myself, I will be overruled. When I allow myself to be used and humiliated, I feel bad about being weak and needing to hold down my resentment, blame and hate.

The only way out of the paradox is through compassionate awareness of how we are perpetuating our own victimhood, clinging to our story, our negativity, our past. Awful things may have happened to us as a child, and even though we are that child no longer we can hold that part of ourselves with utmost tenderness and care, allowing it to grow up under our loving tutelage.

In her TEDx Talk Lesley Quilty speaks of the terrible time when she lost her former husband, the father of her son, her friend. Walking in the garden in a state of desolation, she heard an inner voice, firm and kind: "Say yes. Just say yes – it might seem like the worst thing ever, but just say yes." When she did, she felt herself surrender to life not how she wished it was, but to how it is. Saying "yes", she discovered, presented her with so many more options than when she was locked in a continual internal monologue of no's against the things she didn't want to happen in our troubled world. She came to the point of being able to say "yes" to her past, including the sexual abuse that should not have happened. It had taken her years to understand that it wasn't her fault, that she was not guilty. "Since it did happen," she began to ask, "how has it been useful to me? How did it help me become the person I am becoming, to deepen my compassion as part of all that lives?" In her toolkit, as she describes it, are living in intentional community, friendship, a relationship with nature and a meditation practice through which she has learned to sit and pay attention to all that is arising within and apply compassion to it. She also did hundreds and hundreds of hours of therapy, she says, many ceremonies, many rituals.

Unlike many other people, Lesley Quilty has never minced her words or felt the need to hide her abundant creativity. Quite the contrary: she makes her living being creative. She found her vocation as a clown. Wearing a helmet with goggles and oversized striped trousers over a colourful bathing suit, she loves to make people laugh by poking fun of what we hold most precious. "I am one," she says, "who knows the art of bringing joy and laughter into really difficult situations, the art of playfully naming the unnameable."

Out of the victim role

Half a century ago, Stephen Karpman, M.D, came up with the model of the drama triangle as a way to explain conflicted and intense human interactions. The victim, with a stance of "Poor me!", is described as feeling oppressed, helpless, hopeless, powerless, ashamed and unable to make decisions, solve problems or take pleasure in life. When we take this stance, this theory says, we energetically invite others to step into the roles of persecutor or rescuer. Those three roles make up the drama triangle.

We probably all know how good it feels to come to the aid of someone in need. There is, however, a danger of the rescuer enabling the victim to drown in their misery and keep blaming others. While helping someone, the person in the role of rescuer will at the same time strengthen their negative self-image, as clearly this person cannot fend for themselves. Then co-dependency is around the corner. The third role is the one of the persecutor, who insists with a measure of anger and stern authority that whatever happens is the victim's very own fault, and they should just grit their teeth and get over it.

Drama triangles happen all over the place. We're in them before we know it. They also don't only happen in the outside world. Our inner voices can also shift from one stance to another in a trice. Once we are aware of these archetypal roles we don't need to stay in position. The way out is to step out of the role, whichever one we have taken at the minute. When we move into the middle of the triangle we are neither inferior in a victim role nor superior as a rescuer or persecutor. From the middle we can be neutral observers to what transpires in each of the corners.

The Eastern wisdom traditions recommend compassion as a way out of victimhood. The ancient practice of Tonglen, for instance, is a method by which we breath in the fear, pain and suffering of others, and breathing out send them relief and happiness. As Pema Chödrön points out in her beautiful book *When Things Fall Apart*, the advanced practice of working with compassionate action involves working with ourselves as much as with others. "Being there for someone else," this Buddhist nun and teacher writes, "means not shutting down on that person, which means, first of all, not shutting down on ourselves. This means allowing ourselves to feel what we feel and not pushing it away. To do this requires openness, which in Buddhism is sometimes called emptiness – not fixating or holding on to anything. Only in an open, non-judgmental space can we acknowledge what we are feeling." What she describes is like the centre of the drama triangle. From this open space we can connect to our essence. We can observe what happens rather than take part in the action, and thus stop adding to the drama. The mere act of witnessing what happens inside, and holding feelings with compassion as they come, peak and die down, clears the air.

A healing response

Harry, with his unfinished equal opportunity policy, is gripped by a premonition that something awful might befall him when he shows people what he has written so far. This leaves him no choice but to stall and postpone and, in the process, experience the very humiliation he so badly wants to avoid.

Once we see that this kind of conduct is generated by an early childhood conclusion, we can start to take back power over our lives. When we detect ourselves demonstrating kindness outwardly, while inwardly we are seething with impotence and rage – and craving a bite to eat – we can stop for a moment. We can take a deep breath and, rather than brace ourselves for humiliation, embrace our child inside with all its fears and trepidations. As the adults we are now, we can make ourselves bigger than our feelings, and thus we can let go of the identification. Once we have the presence of mind to take a look at what we feel, we can have our feelings and not be them.

As permission is the central issue in this particular childhood conclusion, we may start by asking ourselves if we are okay with trying a different approach – and then watch our response, which may be the fear of the unknown or an unsuspected attachment to the hell we know. Watching the response, we are already giving ourselves a positive present. We are giving ourselves space and time with no expectation whatsoever of an outcome. We are just there for ourselves. If we can find the patient tenderness with which we watch a puppy dog scramble to its feet, we may adopt it now to watch our own thoughts and feelings. We may bend our knees slightly and consciously connect to the earth, the mother that feeds us. Paying our respects to her, we pay respect to ourselves in this moment of being with thoughts and feelings a jumble. We breathe, we are.

Poet, civil rights activist and role model to many, Maya Angelou was molested by her mother's boyfriend as a young child. Her 1969 memoir *I Know Why the Caged Bird Sings* made literary history as the first non-fiction best-seller by an African-American woman. In the last pages of this gripping book she describes how she had a baby at the age of 16. She sat by his bassinet for hours, absorbed in his mysterious perfection, but she wouldn't touch him. Wasn't she famous for her awkwardness?

One night her mother stepped in. She put the three-week-old baby in her daughter's arms and told her he was going to sleep with her. "I begged in vain. I was sure to roll over and crush out his life or break those fragile bones," Angelou writes. Stiff with fear, she vowed to stay awake, but of course she eventually dropped off. Wanting to make a point, her mother woke her gently in the night, inviting her to take a look. Young mother Angelou was lying on her stomach with her arm bent at a right angle to hold up the blanket as a tent for her baby to sleep in. "See," her mother whispered, "you don't have to think about doing the right thing. If you're for the right thing, then you do it without thinking."

Applying the healing response of paying attention to our inner world, giving ourselves the time and space we need, gathering up courage to show our creativity without wanting to please the powers that be, will help us in knowing that in the end we are free to choose our own path. Ralph Waldo Emerson, of course, put it perfectly: "What lies behind us and lies before us are small matters compared to what lies within us."

We may engage the help of family and friends to point out to us when we are stuck in the rut of old disempowerment. When they let on that they actually find it painful when under the guise of a joke we put ourselves up to be mocked and scoffed, we may feel exposed at first. This is where we can make a conscious choice between perpetuating our habitual conduct or venturing to try new ways. We are no longer the child who couldn't counter adults' adverse acts and blamed ourselves for the unwanted attention. We have the power now to choose how to respond to the feedback we receive. We can either go back into hiding or come out one baby step at a time, face up to the truth of our habitual self-depreciation, and start to change it. We will need time to give space to the realization that indeed, we are not being very kind to ourselves, as we learn new self-supporting behaviours. Trusted others can also remind us gently that it is okay to say "no", to refuse, not to accommodate. We can turn practising our new ways into a game for a while, to help us gain confidence in setting our boundaries and sticking to them.

Once we have gained some experience in giving a healing response to ourselves, we can also radiate it out to others who feel overwhelmed, frustrated and disempowered, who eat to keep their rage down, who forever humour others like faithful dogs that keep wagging their tails however they are being treated. Connecting to ourselves first, we can slow down and show interest without any expectation. We know very well that such a child or adult needs more time than others to be able to make a statement or a choice, and often needs to gather their courage to say anything at all. Having hidden their creative expression and unadulterated love deep inside, the time is long gone that they knew what they wanted and so they will try to have us take the lead. We can convey to such a child that we are fully behind them, whatever they choose. To use a typical Dutch analogy, we can treat them like a tulip in spring that has been buried underground the whole winter and only comes out when the sun is strong enough. We cannot make the tulip grow faster, but we can enjoy every little inch it shows more of itself. This is the theme for all of us who have swallowed our pride, our self-esteem and our rage – to come out of hiding and dare to show ourselves.

Knowing the vast numbers of people hurt by abuse in all its ugly guises, we may want to practise this healing response whenever we are in a crowded place. On a bus or in the supermarket, we can inwardly connect to our creative core and repeat these time-honoured phrases to nobody in particular and to everyone at the same time: "May you be happy. May you be safe. May you be at ease. May you be free from suffering."

Turning this childhood conclusion

Turning the childhood conclusion will help put a stop to the confusing mix of thoughts and feelings that tell us to give in to others at the expense of ourselves and keep quiet. Here the five steps are described in brief.

STEP 1: recognize the thought pattern

Awareness begins with noticing when we hear ourselves consent to something because we think it will make others happy. When we signal that we start to feel resentment, when we start to have recurring thoughts that we are powerless or when we try to make ourselves invisible, that is the time to pay attention. The first step is to begin to watch those negative feelings and thoughts, as they stem from a conclusion we drew when we were small.

STEP 2: shift the focus

We can shift the focus to this moment in time, to the person we have become. We can feel our inner fury and frustration, and realize that this is actually our life force. This is exactly the power we can employ to free ourselves from the bondage of having to dance to other people's tunes. We are a free person, and we are free to value ourselves and our own wishes.

STEP 3: thank ourselves

The recurring feelings and thoughts that we are powerless can be linked back to experiences in which our boundaries were crossed, our privacy was violated. We felt overpowered and outranked at the time, and the intention behind this childhood conclusion was to never have something like that happen to us again. Now we can thank the part of us that, from the perspective of a child, saw submission and passivity as the only possible way of getting through life unharmed. There is no harm at all in expressing gratitude to ourselves for the path we have walked.

STEP 4: invite the anger from back then

More stable now through paying homage to ourselves, we act as a container for the sense of disempowerment we experienced back then. Once upon a time we have allowed things to happen to us because we did not dare to refuse, or did not know how. We will take some time to get in touch with that fear again now. If we can keep this up for a few minutes, the anger, frustration and fear will dissipate and we will come out the other end. This way we reclaim the power to be who we are.

STEP 5: be creative, live our life

Our life is ours and no one else's. We may set the direction, plot the course. We are allowed to make our own creative choices, good and bad, just like everyone else. Opening to what is ours to do in the mix of things, we can make a creative contribution.

The first three steps

Whatever our thoughts try to tell us to the contrary, we are the captain of this ship. We are in charge and so we are free to do – and not do – as we please. We don't need anyone's permission to go our own unique way. By turning our thoughts and feelings of powerlessness, we can reclaim our autonomy.

This takes some practice but once we become aware of the disease to please, we will gain greater access to the creativity that is fully intact under the layers we've cemented around it. Taking all the time we need, we will learn to spot the specific thoughts and tendencies that stem from this childhood conclusion. Maybe they manifest in a certain feeling rather than in well-formulated sentences. We may notice a craving for food when we are about to speak up, and recognize it as an attempt to cop out and soothe ourselves. This childhood conclusion might express itself in a desire to remain invisible in company. We may habitually force ourselves to put up with the scorn of colleagues, like Harry, rather than showing them what we have produced so far.

Going through the steps will not be easy as we have cultivated the habit of swallowing feelings before they can make themselves known. What we can give ourselves to begin with is time. Let's take as long as we need and not be discouraged. It might be a good idea to keep a diary, to jot down each day what feelings we've had that made us go into helplessness and blame. Being honest with ourselves, we can write down without restraint what we think about people who don't take us seriously or make us consent to things against our wishes. We may rant and rave as much as we like on these pages, as we will never show them to anyone. Our ticket to freedom is for our eyes only.

STEP 1: recognize the thought pattern

Once we have developed the habit of capturing what is bothering us, we will notice that we are often grappling with a dilemma: we want to play along as we want the warmth of companionship, but at the same time we don't want to play along as it is not really our game. What to do? If we play along for the sake of not wanting to be difficult, we violate ourselves. If we don't play along, we're afraid we will be humiliated in public.

The first step of turning this childhood conclusion is to realize that we can notice these kinds of thoughts. We can see them, jot them down, become aware of them. Yes, there is a dilemma, and only watching will not solve it, but this is the beginning. Just watch, and see what happens. Let's take note when we get the sense that we're forced to do something because we think it will please others. Let's catch ourselves when we mosey on over to the fridge – what are we up to? Let's stop for a second before putting something sweet into our mouth and ask ourselves what emotion we are trying to avoid feeling. Let's pay attention to when we are sighing or dragging our heels. Becoming aware of all these giveaways is the first step.

STEP 2: shift the focus

In this second step, we are going to shift the focus to the adult we have grown into. We are no longer the child who felt powerless in relation to parents and other adults. We are a creative human being with a heart full of compassion. We are someone who delights in comforting others. We are able to poke fun at life and we are free to lead life our way.

If discouraging thoughts arise within that say this is surely not going to help and we will not be able to do this anyway, let them come and let them go, like planes at the airport. When we travel, we don't go to the first gate and board the aircraft no matter where it is going; we find out where the plane to our destination is leaving from and that's where we go, so that we end up where we want to be. It works the same way with thoughts. We don't have to "board" the first thought that passes by; we can pick the one that takes us where we want to go. Right now we want to focus on who we have become. We have survived ordeals. We have preserved our innate goodness. We are someone who cares. Let's now firmly ground ourselves in appreciation for who, in spite of everything we've been through, we have become.

STEP 3: thank ourselves

You may well think it ridiculous to thank our feelings or thoughts, and you are welcome to think whatever you like. At the same time, you will have to concede that it hasn't really been productive to suppress your anger, resentment and reprehension. With this childhood conclusion, we have banked our disempowerment, our rage and with it our sense of self-worth. We suppressed our life force. We did all this in an attempt to keep the peace. Whether we have succeeded in that pursuit or not is of no importance now. As a child, the intention was to preserve the safety of the family, help create a stable environment, please the people we trusted and loved.

We sacrificed ourselves for that purpose. No one has thanked us for keeping secret what should have come out into the open. They may not even have noticed. They still might not see, but we do now, and so let us thank ourselves. In our own words or with a gesture we may thank the part of us that was not able to stand up to our parents or other adults. We may salute ourselves for bearing the pain that at the time we thought we had to keep to ourselves and do our utmost not to show. That is why we might even thank our rage and resentment; these emotions have consistently reminded us that something was out of kilter.

We may also want to express gratitude for our perseverance, because we survived it all and have become who we are today. All those years we have been doing our utmost to make others happy. That is no small feat and it merits gratitude. This is an excellent time to find words to express this gratitude clearly. "I thank myself for all those times that I did what others wanted and kept my mouth shut. I see how strong I actually was, even when I scolded myself for being weak. I now appreciate and thank myself for all those instances," are the kinds of sentences that we might start with before moving on to finding words of our own.

This might all seem rather strange and thus evoke fear of making another mistake by following someone else's path. Still, my suggestion is to give it a try. Let's begin small and find out what happens when we give ourselves a pat on the back while we're taking a shower: "Well done, you!" In the privacy of the bathroom no one needs to see or hear. This is between us and ourselves, and I bet that literally patting yourself on the back out of appreciation for what you have put up with all these years will make an immediate difference to how you start the day. Thanking ourselves is a first step in regaining our self-respect and beginning to love ourselves again.

Practising these three steps over and over will help us emerge bit by bit out of the hiding place that we have created for ourselves. While it seemed the only way to go at the time, most of us will own up to feeling a sense of imprisonment. We've locked ourselves up and thrown away the key, while in truth we are autonomous, self-ruling, free to shape our lives, just like everyone else. From the vantage point of the adult we have grown into, we can see that now. Let's nurture and grow the inner freedom we feel. Let's feel good about having resisted a bite of food, finished a task – whatever it was that we can set store by today. We can make a positive choice and allow that feeling to expand. We can let a sense of contentment flow through our body and enjoy, as much as we can, this feeling of self-worth and maybe even, who knows, self-love.

Anger as life force

I have yet to meet a person who was taught as a child how to deal with their anger. "Go to your room and come back when you've cooled off," is the marching order most of us received when we lost it. How were we to learn to let our anger flare up, allow it to move through us so it could dissipate? I did a lot of anger-work with clients in my private practice. I would stamp my feet and lift my arms to pull down an imaginary, heavy roll-down shutter while shouting "No!" Many of them have been baffled seeing me, a white-haired woman with pearl earrings, demonstrate how to howl "No" from deep down in the belly. After repeating this exercise a few times they have without exception felt better, stronger, freed up. I have found letting our anger move hugely helpful in avoiding getting stuck in victim mode, in setting boundaries and holding them and, first and foremost, in discovering that anger is life force distorted. Once we get rid of the charge of the anger, the life force starts to flow through unhampered and life takes on a different guise.

A common misunderstanding among people who "work on themselves" is that they need to tell home truths to everyone who has done them wrong in their lives. Yes, we have been hurt, humiliated, abused or in other ways done wrong by, whether consciously or unconsciously. This doesn't mean that we have to speak out to these people now. More often than not such confrontations do not bring the desired results anyway. The other person might go into such a state of shame that we feel as if we have suddenly turned into the persecutor from the drama triangle. They might laugh at us and dismiss our truth as being made up and thus hurt us all over again. Though mediation and reconciliation can be healing, ultimately clearing the air isn't really about the other person but about ourselves. Can we forgive ourselves? Can we appreciate, love and respect who we are and who we have become?

Fully turning this childhood conclusion

The essence of turning this childhood conclusion is that we find the old trepidation, resentment and anger and let them go, so that we will be able to say "no" with confidence wherever we are. This will often need deeper work but turning the childhood conclusion is a good starting point. We can apply it whenever we find ourselves slipping back into old patterns of disempowerment.

We can do step 4 by ourselves but mining deep-seated anger is not easy to do alone. A friend, or a partner if we have one, might be good support, especially if they are willing to begin by stamping their feet on the floor with us so the fire starts to rise in the belly. If it feels awkward to ask someone else to accompany you in this strange activity, you can do it by yourself a few times until you are ready to invite someone else into the process. The invitation can sound as simple as: "I have to blow off steam. Will you join me?" In sports stadiums crowds of thousands perform this act together, so why not do the same in the privacy of your own home? Taking care of our fury in a controlled manner is certainly healthier than eating candy, being grumpy or exploding at innocent bystanders who unintentionally push our buttons. Just make sure you are home alone, or at least in a place where you will not be disturbed and no one can hear you while you are at it.

The ultimate goal of the full exercise is to find our "NO!" Not just a little teeny-weeny, humbly, inaudibly spoken "no" but our "NO!" Not the "rather not but if you insist" but an "Up To Here And No Further!" Our powerful, strong, uncompromising, unrelenting "NO!"

STEP 4: invite the anger from back then

In step 3 we expanded the feeling of self-worth and maybe even self-love. Once we have got a nice flow of feeling good about ourselves going, we can think back to a recent time when we resigned ourselves to a situation, stuffed ourselves with comfort food or put up with much more than we wanted to. This event can serve as the portal through which we can get in touch with our sense of powerlessness, helplessness, despair and self-loathing. As the adult we are now, we can allow the pain to rise from all those times we've been bossed around, had others determine what was good for us, when they came in without knocking and we put up with it; all those occasions when we discounted what we wanted and went along.

As the adult we are now, we can act as a container for all these feelings of resignation, disempowerment, lethargy, self-loathing, fury and hate.

We now take the lid off the pit in which we stored the ire. We don't need to remove it completely right away, just open it a bit for starters. We will allow some of the gall to escape, like steam from a cauldron of boiling water. Steam once powered the engines of factories, trains and ships that went all over the globe; this is the time to feel the power that our anger holds. Grabbing a towel or a tennis racket, we can thump the arm of a chair or a pile of cushions with all our might. Bend the knees, bring the twisted towel over the head, holding it with both hands, and go for it – beat, hit, strike, slap, whack, bang, whip, smack, bash, flog, thump the chosen practice target. Let's not be half-hearted now, but wallop, maul, club, bludgeon with all the power we can muster not only from the torso or arms, but from the whole body. Let the outrage rise up from the belly, open the throat and shout "NO!"

A voice long silenced needs time to gain strength. No one I have worked with has found this process easy or comfortable at first. All the alarm bells of societal conditioning start ringing at even the suggestion of giving the anger free rein. The "go to your room and come back when you've cooled off" conditioning is mirrored by societal norms of frowning on people who lose their composure. The voices of conditioning like to keep us moored where we are. If they start protesting in us now, that is actually a good sign as it signifies that we are stretching beyond where we have previously allowed ourselves to venture. The trick is again to see these thoughts and not go with them. We might even call a halt to them as this is what we are practising anyway: drawing a line in the sand, sticking to our boundaries and not letting anything or anyone keep us from finding our voice. We are putting the habit behind us of others, and our own thoughts, determining our life. Our lives are ours to live.

STEP 5: be creative, live our life

Once we are able to state our "yes" and our "no" clearly, we will immediately see life become simpler. People like Harry will note how their capacity to consult with colleagues grows. He will get back the many hours he previously spent vacillating, and be the kind of accessible manager he likes to be, with an exceptional feel for the needs, wants and talents of his staff.

As we turn destructive anger into constructive life force we will notice that the perennial dilemmas start to dissolve. Our life force will help us do whatever is in our power to alleviate the suffering of others. From a darling person, we turn into a person daring to love. Our creativity, compassion and the gift to connect people can now fully come to life. We have a large capacity to accept people exactly as they are and see the positive in any circumstance. We are second to none in being able to enjoy life. We hold the power over our own life. We are sovereign, we are autonomous, we are free.

A positive present

Transforming anger into life force can be done in many constructive and creative ways other than whacking a cushion. Taking up a sport, hitting or kicking a ball, going swimming, running or dancing are all excellent pastimes that may serve us well in keeping irritation and aggression moving instead of banked. We may just want to go out for long walks in nature. All forms of expending physical energy will do the job, as exercise brings us back in touch with the body and with the life force that flows through us. We may consciously practise replacing the old resigned thoughts with new empowering ones, such as:

POSITIVE SELF-TALK

I take life into my own hands.
I might not exactly know how to move forward but I will find out.

I often need more time than others to make up my mind.
Now I realize that my life is mine to live, I grant myself that time.
I don't need to do anything against my will.
I appreciate myself for who I am.
I am autonomous and free to plot my own course.
Just like everybody else I have my boundaries.
I dare to say "no".
There is nothing I need to put up with.
There is nothing I need to do to please others if I don't want to
*   or if it takes too much out of me.*
I just need to express what lives inside me.
I am a sovereign being, a free person.
I am visible.
I shape my life as I see fit.
I please other people – and myself – by being who I am.
I am able to enjoy life to the full.
I am able to share my innate joy with other people.
I feel free.

The more insight we gain into the reactions and patterns of conduct that stem from this third childhood conclusion, the more we will be able to bring our creativity to fruition. The fear of rejection will not disappear overnight, but at least now we are aware that this is a fear that has its roots in the past.

We have grown up and now it is time to grow the self-image accordingly. Each time we defy the fear of rejection and humiliation, the inner confusion and resentment will decrease. I have seen many people who have taken the reins of their life into their own hands shed weight without following a rigorous diet. When we don't need to keep the anger and frustration down, the need to gobble, glut and gorge dwindles. When we no longer feel the need to make ourselves invisible, the need to wrap our creative core dissipates.

Today is a new day in which we may liberate ourselves and show the world who we truly are. We are free. As the oft-referenced line of the 19th-century poet William Ernest Henley says, "I am the master of my fate, I am the captain of my soul."

4

Noble hearts

CHILDHOOD CONCLUSION

"I must be in control."

NEGATIVE SELF-TALK

"I know what is right, but I could be stabbed in the back by someone I thought I could trust at any moment, so I'd better not trust anyone. I must keep situations and people under control."

CORE GIFTS

passion, chivalry, charisma, integrity

"Name a top restaurant in town and I can tell you the best table in the house as that is where I wish to be seated," states Samuel. "It is not my problem if the table has been reserved. That is for the staff to solve and if they are not accommodating? Fine with me – then I will take my business elsewhere." Samuel lives in a world of winners and losers and he will do what he can to end up on the right side of the scale, but we will see: the enemy to be defeated is none other than himself.

Nicole has had a string of lovers and she is infatuated again. Maybe this is the one. As usual when her first delight wanes, she begins to look at her new man with some suspicion. She waits for the moment he will expect her to iron his shirts or take on other household tasks she has no interest in. A trace of disdain creeps into her voice. She begins a game of push and pull, then lashes out, indicating haughtily that she is done with him. This man, however, does not fall into the trap she has so strategically set. His observant reaction helps Nicole realize manipulation will not bring her lasting love.

People like Samuel and Nicole carefully cultivate the image of being on top of the world. More often than not they truly believe that keeping control and knowing what happens next is what life is all about. This belief makes many of us who have drawn the underlying childhood conclusion succeed well in professional life, but be nonplussed in our love life. A relationship requires trust and surrender – and that is exactly what the fourth childhood conclusion urges us to avoid. We've been so deeply hurt in our youth, we've felt so betrayed in the offering of our pure love to one of our parents, that we resolved never to run the risk of having our heart broken again. "I must be in control and know or, better yet, determine what happens next" is the resulting childhood conclusion. If we can't trust our parents with our love, who can we trust?

Love and trust are the themes of many of the myths and sagas that have been told through the ages. They relate the hero's or heroine's journey to find the holy grail. "Each entered the Forest Adventurous at that point which he himself had chosen, where it was darkest and there was no way or path." Mythology professor, lecturer and writer Joseph Campbell has often quoted Gawain, one of the noble knights of King Arthur's Round Table, in *The Quest for the Holy Grail* by an anonymous 13th-century monk. To this day the tale of how a dashing youngster leaves home on a quest for the truth is a major theme in literature, plays and films.

We love these stories of coming home to ourselves as they remind us of our own quest for the path that is uniquely ours to walk. Through waking up hard from the fantasies of our juvenile heroic games, this childhood conclusion sets us on an adventure in which we discover how we can make our childhood dreams of chivalry and valour come true.

The classic story

Here is how it goes. The girl stands in front of the mirror as her father enters and matches her own admiring looks. "I wish your mother would be as attentive to her looks as you are, my little princess," he says as he strokes her hair. The girl feels seen as the woman she will grow up to become. She feels courted, appreciated and loved, the apple of her daddy's eye. Like a flower opening, she gives herself fully to her father in her fantasy life. Then comes the agony of not knowing how to be with her mother from now on. Fond of both parents, she feels like a traitor while also suspecting that her father is not fully honest in his intentions with her.

Just as many girls have a penchant to aggrandize their role in the lives of their fathers, boys tend to do this in relation to their mothers. "When I grow up, I will marry you," the young boy announces to his mummy. She smiles and asks him if for now he would mind the baby. The boy interprets this request as a confirmation of him being the one responsible for making sure that his mother can work for a few hours. It is him she counts on as his father is away a lot. In his young mind, he starts to see himself and his mother running the household together. He knows exactly when to bring her a cup of tea. She looks up from her laptop with a tender gaze. "Thank you, darling. You take such good care of me." The boy grows a few inches. He feels like a real man who knows how to cater to a woman. Not like his father, who is not around to make her feel prized. No, he is the one who truly cherishes her, and he takes his mother's loving smile as confirmation of their secret bond.

That night the boy wakes up because he hears noises coming from his parents' bedroom. He hears his mother shriek but cannot make out what she is saying. He ran in, once, to save her. He remembers his parents' surprised looks as they said he had better go back to his own bed. Clearly unwanted, he did so, but could still hear them talking in soft voices, and laughing. This time he goes to the bathroom instead, and leaves the door open as he flushes the toilet in a wordless signal that he is awake. Alone in his bed, he feels betrayed. If he is the one taking care of his mother so well, how come she shuts him out as she turns to his father?

Children get entangled in their parents' relationship in all kinds of ways. In unstable partnerships parents will, knowingly or unknowingly, involve their children in the great game of love and power that goes on in the house. A mother may take to cuddling her son excessively as a sly signal to his father that yes, there are still people in this world who value her love. The young son may sense that the cuddling is not really meant for him, but appreciate the motherly advances anyway. Conversely, after a fight with his wife a father might seek out his daughter and tell her that she understands him in a way others don't. With the line between fantasy and reality not clearly drawn at this age, the girl delights in feeling so important to her father. Her mother doesn't really count, she starts to think. She is her dad's true love.

Our young hearts, overflowing with love, are broken when our devotion is not wanted in the way that we thought it was. We've been put on the wrong foot, but we are quick learners of this harsh lesson of life. We will watch our backs from now on. We will do all we can to make sure never to get the short end of the stick again.

Enemy-making

Lots of people feel intimidated by Samuel but his current girlfriend is not among them. Under his bravado, she sees the big heart she fell for the first time they met. She is in love with the man Sam could be, if he dared to live from his heart rather than from the premise that life is a continuous competition that he should win. "His mind is quick to reduce people to enemies," she says, "and then he turns himself into a kind of knight who needs to go into combat. It's quite an exhausting existence – and without wanting to sound naive, this whole enemy-making exercise seems not really necessary to me."

Her childhood conclusions do not lie in the same area as her chosen partner's. Samuel does find her a little otherworldly, but holds her in such high regard that for the first time in his life he wonders if he sees more enemies out there than there are. This totally new thought has him puzzled for a while. He cannot fully place it in the clear-cut categories he usually puts ideas and people in, and he doesn't like what he cannot figure out. Yet, he must admit that he would also like to get rid of the tension that, like an outboard motor on a speedboat, has him rushing through life.

Growing up with this childhood conclusion

Children play games in which without blinking an eye they give themselves and each other the most grandiose roles.

I was a firefighter who saved the children in danger.
I was a doctor who cured everyone who was sick.
I was so famous I could make everyone happy.
I was boss of the whole world!

In this fantasy world of our childhood, we are crystal clear on the difference between the goodies and the baddies. With our playmates we wake the dead, rescue princesses and presidents and save the world from the dire disaster about to strike. We are of royal descent, and although brought up by normal people, one day we will step forth and reveal ourselves as who we truly are. When we grow up, we will marry our lovely mother or our fabulous father, who have not yet lost any of their lustre in our childish eyes. All of this falls easily within the vast realms of possibility. Our fantasy is immeasurable and with no clear demarcation yet between what is true and what is not, misapprehensions originate in real life in the twinkling of an eye.

When we were young we felt completely at one with our parents. We trusted them with our lives. When this trust was broken because of an innocent youthful assumption that we were the true love of one of our parents, we felt wrecked. Apparently, no one is to be trusted, the young child concludes as it nurses its broken heart. From one moment to the next, in our own perception, we have been downgraded from hero to loser. That hurts. As children we were under the impression we occupied a special role for one of our parents. We thought we had read the situation well and had stepped up to the plate. We felt we were saving the day. In one fell swoop all of that is gone. Lost. We ourselves are lost if we allow such a misunderstanding to arise again, is how we try to make sense of what we are feeling. This heartbreak is not a pain that we can possibly go through twice. We simply would not survive. Of course, this is not a logical train of thought. These incidents, however, when as a child we feel betrayed in the relationship with our parents, form the basis for thoughts of distrust and having to call the shots that may become the primary driver in our life.

Those of us who have jumped to this win-or-lose childhood conclusion are easily identified by a strong desire to run the show, a determination to know what happens next, a self-imposed demand for control, compulsive competitiveness and wanting to win. We ache to get the last word in at all times, and if we don't, we will coax and cajole, jockey, manipulate and manoeuvre, leave no stone unturned until our right to speak is acknowledged and we can prove that we were right all along. Smug in our triumph, when all can see that we have the upper hand, we can relax temporarily – but the fight for being first can flare up again at any moment.

We usually don't like being alone and strike up friendships easily. Natural leaders in the class, team or circle of friends, we will determine which game is being played during break-time and later, which pub or club our group will favour. If needs be, we will call the shots by imposing our will, but mostly we are such masters of temptation that friends will realize only later that once again they have done things our way.

Outwardly, as children or teenagers we seem to know no fear. We get into fights, physically in the playground and verbally later and think an assertive, even aggressive approach is normal. We appreciate others standing up for themselves, and don't think twice of taking advantage of those who are not as fast on their feet as we are. We are daredevils who, when caught in the act of transgression, will respond with defiance, making it hard for parents, teachers and other educators to keep us in line. We choose a version of the truth that is to our advantage and are often able to argue our side of a story in such a charmingly convincing manner that we are given the benefit of the doubt. If we cannot save our skin through persuasion, our harsh side may come to light. We may make short work of others and their prim propriety. Regardless of who confronts us, we will wipe the floor with all who stand for upholding goody-two-shoes rules and behaviours. The world is a jungle, we will argue; *we* know better than to believe in a fairytale world where people are honest and trustworthy.

Parents may need to pull out all the stops not to lose their grip on a child like this. Their son's or daughter's disobedience may provoke anger but that will have a counterproductive effect as the child will probably only grin. The one who blows their top loses the battle, is their prevailing attitude. Allowing temper to flare up is a sign of weakness and those who do are losers that this world has way too many of anyway. We will make sure to come out on top, no matter whether this wins us points in the popularity contest or not. That is not our primary concern.

Peers might be intimidated by these young leaders and associate with them because they don't dare to risk their ire. As leaders, these youngsters may be fickle and change the rules from one day to the next, or suddenly make friends with someone previously scorned or ignored. That is one way of putting companions to the test – will they be loyal? If friends meekly follow our lead, they show no spine and cannot truly be trusted. If they resist, they can't be trusted either. This just goes to show that when push comes to shove no one is trustworthy.

At other times, we are the personification of charm and our charisma has people dancing to our tune. The boy is capable of apologizing to the object of his derision in such a disarming way that he is instantly forgiven. The girl winds her parents, teachers and latest boyfriend around her little finger. Full of adoration, he blindly does her bidding. She fully realizes that her little game of manipulation prevents them from having a true relationship, but how to relate to someone on equal footing, she has no clue.

Nothing wrong with children who are keen to win, and in this competitive society they often do well. When, however, winning has turned into a matter of life and death, then we are at the mercy of this childhood conclusion of heartbreak and broken trust. Underreacting from this childhood conclusion might make us seem arrogant, as we pursue our own success without being much interested in how our acts affect others. It's everyone for themselves, we think. Overreaction will show up by rushing forward in time, pushing to keep control over the outcome of proposals, projects, even relationships. We can handle all that comes our way, is the image of worldliness we'll like to project.

Physical tells

The pain in our hearts was once so acute that we swore a holy oath never to allow this to happen again. Henceforth we made our heart into a fortress that is not easy to conquer. We don't literally walk around in chainmail like the gallant knights of the Round Table, but we carry an energetic shield over our hearts. Men will often develop strong necks, broad shoulders and a big torso. In women this shielding usually doesn't show in muscularity as much as in an overall tension in the upper body and the face. We may send out signals of a restrained sexuality, and enjoy the disconcerting effects this has on both men and women.

Living with the distrust arising from this childhood conclusion has us permanently on the lookout for danger from unexpected sources. In order to feel secure, we want to know or determine what happens next. When we cannot see around the next corner, this adds to our stress. The tension generated by this pervading physical sense of unrest will have us habitually bouncing one of our legs up and down or tapping our fingers.

We are intense, wherever we go. We stare people down with piercing eyes. We like to keep a whirlwind pace. We walk ahead, as if in front of the troops, hurriedly as if being hunted, aiming to arrive first. We find it hard to sit still but if we do, we will sit so our back is covered and we have a strategic overview of the space we are in. We hate the controls being in someone else's hands, so we will be nervous before flying and will make sure we are first to get off the plane once it's landed. When on trips with friends, we have been known to play the group dynamic so that we get the best room in the house, the biggest bed, the best seat at the table – preferably at the head. If we cook, we show off. If others cook for us, we will amicably pour the wine and determine the topic of conversation with our loud voice and hearty laughter. We love stories of success and heroism, we love to talk about winning and winners, we like to show off that we are associated with people on the good side of the fence. We are out to play first fiddle when no first fiddles are required. Throwing out controversial statements, we may create two camps when a moment ago there was harmony around the table. Turning a conversation into a competition, we may then debate or seduce and tempt people to come into our corner – and enjoy the game we've created immensely. Going to get bread for the troops early the next morning, we ask for a reduction as a token of appreciation for our custom. Turning a simple transaction into a negotiation is one of our well-tried ways of making contact with people whoever and wherever they are. If they don't play along, we can be harsh. If they do get our game, it is good cheer all around.

A giant chessboard

Meet Andrew, an entrepreneur who has done well for himself. He and his wife both drive convertibles, sport expensive designer clothes and wear watches that cost a workman's annual wage. His children like to entertain him by dishing up stories of how well they do in sports and how they succeed in their studies and jobs. In the kitchen, they confide in their mother about the doubts that go with their age. If Andrew happens upon them during these conversations, he always comes up with a quick fix. To him the world is like a giant chessboard that requires cunning moves and striking when the time is right. He has proven to be a master of this way of operating and expects no less from his brood. That is why he can't stand it when they can't make up their minds and postpone making clear-cut decisions on their no-doubt brilliant futures. This kind of hesitancy irks him no end. "Weigh your options, keep some open while moving full steam ahead" is the motto that has always propelled him. To good effect, too. Success needs organizing.

If you want to come out on top, you must know where you stand, where you want to go and how to pull strings to make it happen. Suck up when needed, overrule when you must. Be generous while keeping count, always negotiate your way and strategically call in favours. That game plan is what got him to where he is today. He is someone in this world. He knows where he stands. People who don't might end up like his ragamuffin brother, the artist, who lives hand to mouth from what he might sell. Andrew shudders at the thought of living such a haphazard existence – and heaven forbid this might be the fate of his kids.

Shining armour

Men talking from the childhood conclusion of control will typically greet friends with a hearty clap on the back, bellowing "Everything under control?" This seemingly simple phrase indicates their state of mind. Wanting to avoid sour surprises at all costs, their primary goal is exactly that – to keep everything under control. They just assume that the same goes for everyone else, and that if you're not aware of treachery going on all the time, you should be. On the basis of this childhood conclusion, many of us develop well-tuned antennae for who holds the power in any given situation, and how to exert influence, manipulate and cash in. Once we develop our own antennae for this part of us that so badly wants the upper hand in life, we see this childhood conclusion approach thrive in areas where power is the name of the game. In politics, in corporate life, in the media, in every circumstance where outsmarting others wins the day.

As long as we are not aware of how this strong identification with having to win and remain in control determines our worldview, we may even not shy away from going beyond the pale to reach our goals. In such instances, we are not overly strict when it comes to the truth and may interpret rules and regulations loosely to our own advantage. A mistake by a cashier will be our gain, as might be inside information on a competitor. Convincing ourselves that we are in the right, we walk a tightrope between what is legally or morally sound and what is less so. Feeling deeply betrayed, some of us may take this up a notch, feeling justified in getting our own back or taking revenge. The armour plating around our heart then serves to close off all feelings for those on the other side and leave us with eyes only for our own gain, position and power. In movies, these extremes are embodied in the Mafia bosses and drug lords who lead a life of luxury, yet are imprisoned in their own expansive villas, surrounded at every step by bodyguards whom they are never sure they can trust. Even their loved ones they trust no further than they could throw them. A house of cards, indeed.

Talking about movies: the young child thought him or herself a hero and this intention to make life better for people and save the world is essentially unchanged in adulthood. All stories in which an average person steps forth and through their courageous acts turns out to be a hero, or in which a heroine defies the bad guys to find her true love, appeal to our imagination. We recognize this impetus to save the day. In truth, that is our most precious dream. We may not trust anyone, we may always scheme and strategize, we may want to be right at all costs, yet in our heart of hearts what we truly want is to do good for the people we love.

Negative self-talk

Despite the outer sheen of self-confidence, we cannot help but notice we are as tense as a bowstring, for the simple reason that life tends to take unpredictable turns. Accidents happen, disease and disaster strike, people certainly don't always march in the direction we would like them to; thus, being in control is elusive. Dominated by this childhood conclusion, the negative self-talk will tend to sound like this:

NEGATIVE SELF-TALK

People seem kind enough until they suddenly turn against me.
I don't trust anyone.
Trusting others is for the losers, the naive.
My experience tells me we can never truly rely on anyone.
I'd better keep my cards close to my chest.
I have to be able to control a situation.
I must be in the driver's seat.
I will be a winner in life.
I will save the day and protect what is mine.
If I don't hold the reins, I don't know where I stand.
That leaves me exposed and feeling vulnerable – defenceless even.
Attack is the best defence.
I must make sure to have my back covered at all times.
I must make sure to come out on top.
Life is about making sure you're in control.

I always look to be in a position of power.
This helps me be ahead of unexpected change.
Also, this helps me keep others out of harm's way.
As long as I am in charge, nothing will go wrong.
I have my life in order and that is not something everyone can say.
I hate losing.
Who doesn't win, doesn't count.
Losers are the underdog.
I'd rather remain in control.
If others don't see things my way, I will use my powers of persuasion.
If people stand in my way, I will take my revenge.
Those who don't want what is good for me, are out – I will make
    sure of that.
I need to win the battle or I will move away.
I notice people seeing me as overbearing and bossy.
What I want more than anything else is to love people and to
    safeguard those I love.
For love I need to open my heart.
I like to play the part of the hero but opening my heart is what
    I fear the most.

Core gifts

In our youthful fantasy games, we were passionate about saving the starving animals, the sick children, the whole wide world. We were ardently in love with one of our parents. Behind our gruff or seductive adult demeanour this fierceness is still fully alive and kicking. This zeal makes us throw parties everyone wants to be invited to, forge strategic business deals for the company we work for, lead teams to achievements beyond their wildest imagination as we set an inspiring example of driving ourselves to the limit. Once we are over having to prove ourselves right all the time, our zest will allow us to move mountains for a good cause. We believe in the people we love with a vengeance, and they are many. With our whole heart, we want only the best for them.

Courage has the French word for heart in it, *coeur*, and this quality rides right alongside our passion. We weren't afraid when we were young and we still aren't. We have the courage to speak up for what we believe in. To us this is obvious and we cannot imagine how other people would not have the amounts of natural fortitude that we have always possessed as just a part of our make-up.

We know how to charm people into doing things just the way we like them. We are the handsome ones, dressed to impress, who chivalrously hold the door for the old lady to pass through. We sweep everyone off their feet with our dazzling smile so, of course, they listen to our take on what needs to be done and agree to our leadership. Those who make it to high posts in society cannot do so without an ample dose of charisma. They need to be able to convince colleagues or voters of their trustworthiness, even when all of us know that in complex situations they will have to compromise and go against why we voted them in.

Integrity is, ultimately, the highest good we know. We may make things happen with our passion, courage and charisma, but having integrity is ultimately what makes us feel good about ourselves. We can, unobtrusively when needed or through overtly exercising power, influence a course of action, but if we are completely honest with ourselves, we want nothing more than to be congruent with our values. From a black-and-white childhood view of goodies and baddies, we have discovered that in order to do good we sometimes had to be bad. We have confused dedication with love, and unrequited eros with rejection. We were young knights, heroines, royals, and these archetypes are still very much alive within us. Our integrity is like a compass showing us where to use our formidable skills to fight a worthy cause.

Talents honed

Not wanting to be caught on the back foot ever again, we have developed our strategic insight so we can entertain several scenarios of what is coming all at the same time. We don't need a flipchart to have an overview of the future as it might play out; all potentially unfolding options are as vivid and real in our heads as is the person standing next to us. As things change in the outer world, as they are wont to, we change the inner strategic images and plot our course of action accordingly.

We are the best project managers, executives, entrepreneurs and strategists, who can wheel and deal with people at every level of the societal ladder. We know how to create an atmosphere conducive to achievement. Conditioned as we are to go for winning, once we have regained access to our hearts we will be able to shift perspective and not begrudge others their victories. We thoroughly enjoy the matching of powers, of determination, of clever argument.

Once we are free of needing to be right, we will take our hat off to the last man standing, pay homage where homage is due and learn a trick or two that might come in handy next time.

The paradox of trust

People like Samuel, Nicole and Andrew are masters at playing the game of power but actually, deep down, they are tensed up and scared. They are terrified that one day someone will come around who is faster, smarter and more skilful than they are, and they will have to relinquish their place in the sun. They dread that after all is said and done, in spite of all they achieve in their lives with their charm and strategic insight, they will still turn out to be the ones who are not to be trusted. It is true they often act out of calculation, they are opportunistic and they make others do their dirty work for them. Driven by passion, they may be utterly sincere in their love for their partner – and adulterous at the same time. They know how to make amends so they are quickly forgiven, but in essence that is not what this is all about. The paradox underlying this childhood conclusion is about love:

THE PARADOX
My pure love having been betrayed once, I aim to protect myself by anticipating what may happen and controlling what does, but living like this prevents me from truly loving again.

To stop fighting is the huge challenge these people face. The enemy to be defeated turns out to be none other than ourselves. Love may flow freely again once we learn to bow our heads to the mystery of life, to the unpredictability of people and the love we feel in our own hearts. The paradox here is that it takes a hero's courage to surrender and that braving it will turn us into the noble and chivalrous person we have always wanted to be.

The inner opponent

William "Bill" Ury has worked with parties in conflict, both in business and politics, all over the world. His passion is to get people to agree in complicated corporate and international warlike situations, as he states in a talk he held at Google's Cambridge offices at the beginning of 2015. I read his first book *Getting to Yes* in the 80s when he and his colleagues had just founded the Program on Negotiation at Harvard. Its elegant description of the deeper layers under our apparent demands in a negotiation has always stayed with me. The central tenet of the Harvard Negotiation Project is that most negotiations involve not only the outcome but also the relationship between parties. Curbing our own reactions while listening for what the other side really wants makes for solutions that allow both parties to leave the negotiation smiling.

Authority no longer being what it was in the old days when parents, teachers and bosses issued orders for children, students and employees to carry out, the amount of time we spend on getting to agreement has only gone up. Asked which negotiations people find the most challenging, those with external people like customers or those with internals ranging from spouse and kids to colleagues, most say the latter. The more internal, the more difficult, is what Ury found in over 30 years of studying, teaching and applying negotiation skills. Only recently did he realize that his first book needed a prequel, as the most difficult person in any negotiation is ourselves, so he wrote *Getting to Yes with Yourself*.

As an example Ury relates how a former president of Venezuela shouted at him for hours about the troubles in his country and the traitors seeking his demise. While internally going through all the feelings of anger and anxiety of potentially seeing two years of work done in this country go down the drain, Ury pinched the palm of his hand and wondered what it was like to be in this president's shoes. He listened with such attention that the president finally asked him what he should do. "Call a truce over Christmas," Ury said, "have everyone take a break from the adversities and celebrate with their families. They may come back to the table in a different mood." After Ury had listened with empathy to Chavez, Chavez listened to him.

Another example he gives is that of the Brazilian billionaire who had built his fortune from nothing and had got into a bitter dispute with his former business partner. Ury asked the old tycoon what he really wanted. The man surprised himself when he said he didn't want to win the formidable battle as much as he wanted freedom to pursue new business interests and spend more time with his family.

"Who can give you that freedom?" the master mediator persisted. "Are you a complete hostage to your former business partner or can you give this sense of freedom to yourself?" The 40 international top lawyers assembled for the arbitration of the century between these two titans could go home as the tycoons settled their dispute granting each other freedom and respect.

"Going to the balcony" Ury calls this skill of not engaging in the fight, not reacting to anger or accusations, not trying to rationalize with someone in a worked-up state of emotion, but taking a step back from the situation. "From the balcony," he says, "you can overlook the stage and postpone engaging. Some do it by writing an angry email and saving it as a draft, by going for a walk or a cup of coffee with a colleague. Many sleep on it. I pinch my palm as someone once suggested to me."

A healing response

Neither domination nor seduction bring true connection, which is what we long for. We are acting on the basis of the fourth childhood conclusion when we are trying to pick a fight with someone and, like an attorney before their first case in court, we keep single-mindedly rehearsing the same arguments. With repetition our feeling that we are right becomes more resolute, and the adversary more contemptible. We feel superior because we are winners and we feel tense because we don't know exactly what is coming next.

In all these instances, and many more, we can remember that the repetition, the venom, the uncompromising thoughts that paint us unequivocally as the noble warriors are all signs that we're in the constricted space of a childhood conclusion. Once we realize this, we can begin to bring things back into proportion.

From the balcony, as Ury suggests, we can hear ourselves out to find the core of the antagonistic argument. What is it we truly want? Do we dare to feel that in our heart of hearts all we want is to love and be loved in return? Conceding this yearning to ourselves, even if reluctantly at first, will bring palpable relief to our tense muscles. It might bring heartache as well; but by laying a hand on our heart we can quietly feel the childhood pain of loss while conveying to ourselves how strong and brave we have been. We ourselves can send all the love we have to the heartbroken child we once were.

By consciously sending our energy inwardly rather than outwardly, we can calm down and slow down. Breathing deep, we can even admire the skill of our inner litigator building a case, while opening our hearts so wide that the aggressor part of us falls into a warm bath of trust and love. We can send the energy that we usually store in the upper part of our bodies downward into our bellies and our legs. We don't need to be overbearing now. There is no one to be dominated or eliminated so we may come out victorious. Citing William Ury once more, "How can we really expect to get to yes with others, particularly in challenging situations, if we haven't first gotten to yes with ourselves?" Giving ourselves this healing response will help us grow the trust in ourselves, in others and, finally, in life itself.

Conversely, when someone with this childhood conclusion is picking a fight with us with the aim of proving us wrong, a natural tendency might be to get angry, to push back – but this will land us in a fight we don't necessarily want to be in. Neither will it work well to retreat as we will then be considered a pushover. We may tend to ignore what is happening and carry on as normal, but this will provoke even more aggression. As Barbara

Brennan writes in her second book *Light Emerging*, we might not be able to curb the instant defensive reaction when we are under attack.

Her expert advice is to take a deep breath, once we have gone through the initial fight, flight or freeze reactions, bend the knees to help our centre of gravity stay low like that of an immovable sumo wrestler and concentrate on ourselves. We might need to break eye contact to do this; if our counterpart demands we look at them, we can explain that we want to concentrate to take in what they say. This will throw them off guard somewhat as they will have expected a counter-attack, not a dedicated effort to listen to their point of view.

By giving attention to their arguments and not engaging emotionally, we shift the playing field. Mastery is when we can keep our hearts wide open and see the broken-hearted child inside the woman or man trying to needle us. As we concentrate on the anguish below their argumentation or manipulation and listen for the kernel of truth in their accusations, we can have our hearts reach out to theirs. As we register their passion underneath their apparent need to be right, we defuse the energy. We might go as far as to invite them to say more about what gets them so worked up; go into their feelings, while keeping ourselves as calm witnesses of their childhood wounds playing up.

A healing response also works in situations where we are not directly confronted. The person next to us on the underground might be fidgety. Realizing we have no idea what is going on in their life, we can wordlessly give them a healing response as we breathe in, cast our eyes downward and repeat to ourselves the mantra that all is very, very well.

Winning love

Somehow Nicole can't help herself. As with previous boyfriends, after a while she starts to nag her present beau Joe. Any excuse will do. This time she is badgering him about not liking her friends while, she comments, his pals are not exactly world champions. Up until now the men in her life have been wont to defend themselves and their mates. Usually after a fierce fight Nicole would feel highly charged and the make-up sex would be better than ever. The nagging, however, also heralded the end of the rosy first phase of love and the relationship would go downhill from there.

Nicole is astounded when Joe only looks at her as she begins her spiel.

"What are you looking at me like that for?" she snaps at him.

"What is bothering you?" he asks calmly and with some concern.

After a few exchanges of "What do you mean?" and "Nothing but…" Nicole sits down and Joe serves her an immaculate cappuccino.

"Doesn't it bother you when I trash your friends?" Nicole asks.

"What bothers me is that you seem unhappy," Joe replies.

Nicole looks at him quizzically. She? Unhappy? Who does he think he is? Immediately her anger flares again. "Are you mad?"

How he does it she has no clue but Joe remains unabashed.

"Totally," he says with a grin. "I am madly in love with you!"

Her anger dissipates. "You may be on to me," she concedes after a while. "I'm scared that you will not be able to handle me and so I pre-empt your drifting off by trying to fend you off, even if this is not at all what I want to be doing. Ouch, this is hard to confess."

Joe seems to be a pro at "going to the balcony". Other men have come into my private practice saying: "At work I am Superman but in love I am a dodo. I don't know how to relax when I am with someone I like. I order them around as if they are a subordinate, I am not really interested in taking part in their life, I want them to wear sexy clothes so I can show them off. It's come to the point where I just go for one-night stands because I don't want to deal with the hassle of a relationship. Yet I want a wife, a home, a family. What is life worth without others to care for?"

Held hostage by this childhood conclusion, women are apt to go the way of the temptress. Some don't think twice about getting what they want through sharing their beds. They are seductive and create a sexual tension that makes other women suddenly feel boring or unattractive.

We may be familiar with this kind of behaviour in ourselves or others, and realize that through the art of domination or seduction we've once again entered the arena of the never-ending fight. True love, however, is not based on one overruling, manipulating or submitting the other. A relationship is an equal affair.

Turning this childhood conclusion

Being courageous and opening our hearts again, trusting ourselves, others and life. It may sound like a tall order but we are up to the task. The five steps of turning the childhood conclusion help us do that.

STEP 1: recognize the thought pattern

Seeing ourselves from the balcony we can look out for all those times when we think we have to save the day and when the passion for winning and being in control consumes us.

We can begin to pay attention when we wield our considerable charm to bend others to our will. The first step is to see through all of these thoughts and feelings, and become aware that they stem from the childhood conclusion we drew when young.

STEP 2: shift the focus

Bringing ourselves fully to the present moment, we can appreciate how beneath the strategic self we are still someone who wants to be there for others, care for them, share their life and love them to bits.

We have often been the ones to set the pace, to lead the pack and we may honour ourselves now for this quality. We are able to motivate others to bring the best of themselves to life. We are winners, yes, but we are eager to have others share in our good fortune. We may be bossy, demonstrative and extravagant at times, we are also just and generous. Let's feel good about ourselves for all that we bring to whomever we meet.

STEP 3: thank ourselves

The recurring thought pattern of having to come out on top originates from misreading our role as a child. We jumped to the conclusion that from now on we had to anticipate life. Now is the time to give thanks to the part of us that, as a child, saw forethought and control as the only means to prevent future pain.

STEP 4: invite the heartbreak from back then

Fortified by our self-appreciation, we invite the pain we suffered back then. We were heartbroken when we found out we were not the true partner for our father or mother. Together with this grandiose dream, our heart was in smithereens, and this is a pain we can still feel today. It will only last a few minutes.

STEP 5: live a life of trust

We have a huge heart that we can open to everyone we hold dear. Keeping life under control is mission impossible. Being trustworthy and trustful is an art to be cultivated throughout life. Once we commit to this heart and soul, we will be able to co-create with life, dance with the stars and achieve our dreams.

The first three steps

Between the supposed white of winning and black of losing there is a world to be won, if we dare to take a second look at our controlling or manipulating ways and see if there is a more relaxed, connected and collaborative way of achieving our goals. When we catch ourselves feeling captivated by the urge to domineer or prove others wrong, these three initial steps allow us to take a break from our usual comportment and grow our faith in life.

STEP 1: recognize the thought pattern

This childhood conclusion "I must know what lies ahead and be in control" is at the base of observing and predicting other people's course of action. This well-cultivated capacity can now be applied to gauge our own thoughts and feelings. Directing the gaze not outward, to keep track of the movements of others, but inward to what goes on inside of us, we will become conscious of all those times the thought arises that we need to save the day.

We will begin to recognize the compulsive feeling or thought that we have to win, no matter what. We will start to identify the inner strategist who is always a few steps ahead of reality. We may become aware of the stress coursing through our own body, twitching our leg. What is happening right now that makes us tense? By going to the balcony – silently, no one needs notice a thing – we will begin to see how a childhood conviction from way back is running us today.

STEP 2: shift the focus

Watching from the balcony puts a distance between the action on the stage and the one watching. Grounding ourselves in the latter position, we may feel our heart, our leadership and our courage to act. We are a person of passions and this we will remain; ardent lover, sports enthusiast, friend for life. Our will to win, no matter what, was kindled once by the grandiose thought that we would be fully there for one of our parents.

That intention and devotion are still alive within us. In our heart, we are driven by a longing to help people, to be of service, to make a difference. We can bring images of our childhood games back to life: we cured all children and saved the world. Feeling that fervour again for all those worthy causes from our young years, we may now bring in our strategic qualities and our capacity to galvanize people into action. We are not going to lose out here. On the contrary, by opening and following our heart again, we only stand to gain.

STEP 3: thank ourselves

We are warriors, heroines, fighters. The irony is that battling our thoughts gets us nowhere. They are like ever more heads sprouting from a mythological dragon that can never be slain. We are also chivalrous characters, so we can explore gratitude as a way of dispelling our endless thoughts of being under threat. Buddhists bow. Not once or twice, but thousands of times. They are not bowing to any god but to enlightenment, or the Buddha nature that is our original self. This is also good medicine for win-or-lose thought patterns.

Bowing the head is an acknowledgement that all manipulation, controlling, cajoling, negotiation, commanding, seducing and smart-alecking doesn't lead to the deep mutual trust and love we long for. We nurtured this behaviour when we nursed our broken heart. We resolved at the time that we were never going to be afflicted with such pain again. We would never lose out any more. Now we can thank this heroic child who we were, the one who made this decision that would reach so far into the future. We can take our metaphorical hat off to ourselves for how we have conducted ourselves in order to avoid getting hurt. We can salute and honour and pay tribute to that part of our consciousness that knew no better than to close and armour the heart.

This step – thanking the childhood conclusion – may seem to be just the kind of thing losers might be deceived into doing. We might wave this practice away and move on. This might, however, find us forever caught in the grip of the thought that no one is to be fully trusted. Why not take a risk and see what happens when we thank the part of us that for long years attempted to arm ourselves against disappointments in the realm of love? We can do this right here and now, out loud or silently: "Thank you for your endeavour to protect me from being heartbroken again. Thank you for making me a strategist, a winner." We can all make up our own versions of these phrases to appreciate the skills this strategy has brought us that we may continue to apply today. The experience at the root of this childhood conclusion has definitely not broken us, but made us who we are.

The Angel of Trust

Every childhood conclusion has a pearl hidden in its folds, and pearls, as we know, are made from the oyster's tears. The world can be our oyster when we move through the issue of the wounded heart, and find deep trust again.

I count myself lucky to be working closely with one of the originators of the Transformation Game, Kathy Tyler, since she has become a member of the Board of Trustees of the Findhorn Foundation, which I currently chair. Together with Joy Drake she created and developed the inspiring board game in the late seventies whilst they were both living in the Findhorn community. Little did they know that their inspired creation would take them all over the world to host workshops and train facilitators. Thousands have now experienced the unexpected ways the game offers to transform key issues they are grappling with in their lives. Insight cards, received as players move along their life path throwing the dice, bring awareness. Setbacks show where inner work is to be done and angels reinforce inner qualities that can be engaged with in order to realize the intention each player sets at the beginning of the game.

It so happened that as I was working on this chapter, I received their company newsletter with a lovely piece on the angel for the month. It was Trust. "There is a deep rhythm that moves through all life that cannot be controlled by our will," writes Kathy in a reflection on this quality. "When trust informs our experience, it allows our psyche to relax and our soul to be at peace with our situation. We can rest in unquestioned confidence that the universe provides, that we have and will receive what we really need. In fact, often beyond what we alone are even capable of imagining. Trust is the soul's way of attuning to the fundamental laws of reality."

Seen in this way, trust is raised from the daily deliberations of whether we can or cannot trust other people and their capricious nature to the wider context of trust in life, in the universe itself. Kathy continues: "When we have a lot of basic trust, we are courageous and take risks. We don't suppress our competencies. We engage in life wholeheartedly, doing what feels appropriate with the confidence that it will work out. Life becomes a story of creation, not an obstacle course." She also paints the opposite picture: "Without basic trust, we tend to react to what arises in accordance with our conditioning, wanting our life to go one way or another. We cling to predetermined assumptions and outcomes. We become tense and contracted and do all we can to manipulate the circumstances to fit with our desires. Why not," she ends her message, "move from a place of knowing within you rather than as a result of adaptation to outer experience. Let go of your assumptions and need to control life's creative process." Why not, indeed.

Fully turning this childhood conclusion

Turning the thoughts that dominate us from the black-and-white childhood conclusion is helpful. Enduring change, however, comes only with the practice of going through all five steps. In order to gather data before diving in, it might be an idea to ask trusted people how they experience us. A car is fitted with mirrors so we have the fullest possible view while driving. Likewise, a human being at regular intervals needs to ask a friend to function as a mirror, so we get a picture of what we can't see by ourselves. We may need to gather some courage, since to make such a request might be our worst nightmare. Us? Asking someone else to give us feedback on our way of behaving? Alas, as with the other childhood conclusions: the only way is through. The one action we are averse to doing is exactly what is required. The particular portal we will have to go through is taking others into our confidence. Genuinely valuable are those moments when we are truly in contact with another human being. Below the bravado that is what we crave. Let's take the biggest risk we can and ask our partner or good friend when they have felt dominated, outwitted, manipulated, needled, finagled, tempted, bamboozled or even conned by us. Most probably they will be able to give us a few examples that show what we do without being conscious of it. That is information we can work with in step 4 with the aim of restoring our trust.

STEP 4: invite the heartbreak from back then

Our heart may be armoured but we have grown up and become who we are. Revisiting the first three steps without judgement, we identify the pertinent patterns of thoughts and behaviours, shift the focus to who we have grown into and thank ourselves for the way we have survived our broken heart. This makes it easier to get in touch again with the passion beneath. We can call forth a situation in which we felt the control slip away, feel how we felt when this happened. It doesn't need to be anything big. It can be as mundane as going out with friends and being determined to get them to go to the club you like, where you've always tipped the waiters well so they would remember you the next time.

We may recall a time when we felt a fool as we had imagined ourselves playing the hero's part but then painfully discovered that others were already in charge of whatever it was we perceived as an emergency. Or a time when, in unabated fear of betrayal, we were deceived by a lover, a friend or a business partner. In the mind's eye, we may review other recent instances in which the urge for control dictated our conduct and in which, if we're a hundred per cent honest, we actually felt under threat.

The urge to be in the driver's seat is an automatic response to that early moment when we felt betrayed by one of our parents or another adult who was important to us. Becoming aware of how lonely and lost we felt in that instance, we can now relive that heartbreak. We can allow that old pain and grief, or a more recent one, to flow from the heart through the whole body. As the adults we have become we don't need to identify with this pain, we can contain it, however much it hurts. We will not die a hero's death. What will die is the heroic illusion that we will have to keep life under our thumb or else… What will come to life is trust.

STEP 5: trust life, and be trustworthy

A sailor has no control over wind or waves but can become a cunning seafarer who knows how to navigate the elements. Similarly, when we begin to trust others more than we used to, we will begin to live more in the present than in the future that we have sought to outjockey and outguess. People and situations cannot help but change all the time.

Once we have faith in life, the tendency to prove ourselves constantly, to spin the truth our way or put ourselves in a superior position will steadily diminish. The need to build scenarios for all that might happen or go wrong will subside over time, without us losing the ability to use this skill at will.

What joy to be in the fullness of the present moment, to be able to gauge what is happening and participate in shaping what comes next instead of trying to prevent or propel it! Without losing any of the strategic acumen we have developed over the years, the focus will be on how we can allow others to shine. With a more heartfelt approach replacing the previous commanding bossiness, true contact with our dear ones will increase. This, in turn, will provide greater awareness of the effects of our bearing on others. Leadership that attempts to make life better for everyone involved makes for positive collaboration.

It's teamwork that makes the dream work, as they say. Becoming more reliable and trustworthy will make us feel better about ourselves. We have a heart of gold and with trust restored there is a world to be won. Let's go ahead and be as noble as the heroes in the movies we all like to watch.

A positive present

Gradually coming to trust ourselves, other people and life in general, we will trade the old pushy combative projections for positive thoughts like these:

POSITIVE SELF-TALK

I am like everyone else with my strong and weak points.
I like to live from my heart.
I love with my whole heart.
I trust the decisions made by my loved ones, even if they wouldn't be my way to go.
Differences make life interesting.
I make my strategic insights available.
Not to win but to help people find their own way.
I want to help build things.
I feel my passion, my intention to contribute to a good life for other people.
I am pained when I see other people struggle with issues I could solve for them.
I only want what is good for those around me.
For the whole world, really.
That is what I give my all to.
With all the energy and power that is in me.
I am trustworthy.
Life is good, I love it.
I am good, I love.

Andrew is gobsmacked when his wife says that she can no longer stand hearing their children brag about their successes to him while they pour their hearts out to her. He was under the impression all was well in his beloved family. "Yes, darling," she says, "but they are also at an age of making life choices and they could really do with your insight and support. What if next time you didn't shut them up with your solutions but listened to what they are grappling with?" As they discuss the subject, and because she is the one person he trusts in this world, Andrew starts to accept his wife's claim that he has begun to believe that it is his way or no way. For the first time in his life he puts question marks on thoughts that up until now he has held to be absolute truths. "If they don't follow my strategy, they will go nowhere", under the tutelage of his wife becomes, "I want to enter into frank and open-hearted conversations with my children."

As Andrew goes into listening mode, to his delight his children turn out to be fascinating young adults. He discovers that they are remarkably realistic in their appraisals of themselves and their potential. He also finds out that people their age can offer him fresh perspectives on what is going on in today's fast-paced world. One of his daughters confides that she has been to see a psychologist and ventures to suggest he do the same. "I am not so befuddled I would need one of those hand-knitted sweaters," reflex has him say. When he sees her recoil, he grins sheepishly, "Sorry, sweetheart, I did not mean to imply you are befuddled. Not at all." Andrew cannot bring himself to ask his daughter to tell him more about the therapy she is seeking, but he has in his way apologized to her, for the first time she can remember. "I will talk about it with your mother," is as far as he can go for now, adding an endearing attempt to make amends, "only because you say so."

At work, afraid to be scolded for not performing, Andrew's staff have learned to withhold information that their tempestuous boss would rather not hear. As his attention span increases, though, he is being told more and is able to apply his strategic ingenuity to where it is needed most. Unbeknownst to everyone but his wife, he follows his daughter's advice, even though he shudders at the idea that people might find out he is seeing a therapist to talk about his feelings. As time goes by, his staff develop the habit of consulting him more often, and generally come away feeling the better for it. From an exacting entrepreneur who had to win no matter what, Andrew gradually turns into an exacting mentor. He cuts no slack and demands top-notch performances from everyone, but the way he does this now is testimony to his big heart that would have everyone healthy, fulfilled and happy.

5

5

An authentic fit

CHILDHOOD CONCLUSION

"I must conform to fit in."

NEGATIVE SELF-TALK

*"I must observe the norms of those around me, do as they see fit
and put in a perfect appearance. People expect me to know what
I'm doing but I don't have a clue. I don't amount to much and
will soon be found out as a fake."*

CORE GIFTS

eye for essence, unconventionality, ingenuity, authenticity

"You were always a bit off," my 89-year old mother says with relish each
time we revisit what she calls the best time of her life, the years we as
her four children really needed her. "You never quite fit in, not with the other
children, not with us." She presents this without judgement, as a humorous
perception that she made long ago and has never altered. I used to feel hurt
by this depiction but have come to see how accurate her observation is. I tried
to make myself fit the happy-go-lucky way in which she ran our family, but
with different inner values, interests and priorities all I did was play-acting. I
became very good at being appropriate, the well-dressed eldest daughter, the
accomplished hostess, while I slowly lost the awareness of who I truly was.

I have since come to know that a good many of us have the vague notion
that somehow or other life is passing us by. At a tender age, we were seized by
all kinds of sensations in the body that we couldn't name or place. Our parents or their new partners, siblings or educators might not have been appro-

priate in their response to our budding sexuality. Alternatively, we might have felt that, with our set of values, we were wired differently from the rest of the family and we have jumped to the conclusion that we were off the charts and had to adapt to their views and way of life. As a result of drawing this childhood conclusion, we feel we are not fully participating in life but gauging it from a certain distance. We perceive an emotional richness in others that we are unfamiliar with in our own inner life. We entertain a lingering suspicion that we live only on the surface, as if we were cardboard characters modelled on an unattainable ideal. We are convinced we must be missing out on something that makes living worthwhile, without knowing what it could be, as we are constantly adapting as best we can to those around us. We perform well but are convinced that all our achievements are due to luck and one day soon people will be on to us and see that we don't really amount to very much.

Strange and clumsy

Fitting in is a big theme in many people's lives. Years ago, four of us talked about this in the car on the way back from a conference. "I am a redhead. I always stood out as a child," one of us said. "My parents moved a lot so I was always the new kid who never fit with any of the existing groups," said another. "I was born in a family of sports people," the third quipped, which made us laugh – we knew her resistance to any kind of athletic activity. I, of course, was considered "a bit off" by my own mother. This conversation happened 15 years ago but it has stayed with me as a mark of how we each had felt lonely in our "otherness", and how invisible this theme usually is as we give the impression of fitting in so well.

Spending our young years as a cub in a litter, fitting in is vital. We need the support of a family to grow up in, a structure to get us on our feet. It is only logical that children who, like apples, fall a bit further from the tree easily get the eerie feeling that something might be wrong with them. This is the ground for the conviction that we should be different than we are, we should adapt and conform, push ourselves into a box to fit in. When we do, we lose touch with who we really are.

A secret life

In her book *Dying To Fit In*, Erica McKenzie shows how far trying to conform can make us go. She was bullied in high school for being fat, by the popular girls with their seemingly perfect bodies. While her mother tried to convey to her that she was beautiful, young Erica found relief in bulimia, purging her loneliness and despair along with her food. Keeping the secret even from her husband, she started to take weight-loss drugs after the birth of their first child. For nine lonely years Erica continued with the diet drugs, hyper with energy, barely eating or sleeping. Her resulting near-death experience made her see that what others think of us is of no importance when we are at one with ourselves. She has now stopped pretending to be other than she is.

Award-winning actress Natalie Portman gives another example. At the age of 18, having already starred in movies for seven years, she went to Harvard University. In her commencement speech at her alma mater, she talks about how she tried to fit in as a child by adapting her accent, how she was convinced that a mistake had been made when she was admitted to Harvard, or that she had only got in because she was famous. It had taken her a long time, she said, all the way up to her Oscar-winning performance as a ballerina in *Black Swan*, to become immune to what others think and say. "Owning your own experience," she says, talking fast to get out everything she wants to convey to the graduates, "is what that film is about. The character Nina is only artistically successful when she finds perfection and pleasure for herself, not when she is trying to be perfect in the eye of others." She urges her audience not to conform to someone else's values but to follow their own path. "Even if it is strange and clumsy, the reward is making your internal life fulfilling." She has since gone on to portray Jackie Kennedy, who played the role of First Lady to perfection even before orchestrating the funeral of her assassinated husband, President John F. Kennedy, so he would be remembered as one of the greats.

Chris Sacca, a mega-successful investor in start-ups, takes it one step further in his commencement speech at the Carlson School of Management in Minnesota. "The most important piece of advice I can give you on the path to happiness is not just be yourself, but be your weird self. It takes too much energy to be anything but your weird self. Forget what other people think. Everyone here is weird, admit it. We each have our quirks. Celebrate those, be goofy, tell corny jokes, dance awkwardly, express your half-baked thoughts and laugh about your failures."

Owning our experience and being our own weird self is easier said than done. Researcher and author Brené Brown addresses this issue, too, in her best-selling book *The Gifts of Imperfection*. "Like many of you, I'm really good at fitting in. We know exactly how to hustle for approval and acceptance. We know what to wear, what to talk about, how to make people happy, what not to mention – we know how to chameleon our way through the day." One of the biggest surprises in her years of research on wholeheartedness, however, was learning that fitting in gets in the way of being loved for who we are.

In a nutshell, that is the predicament of those of us who have drawn the childhood conclusion that as we need to fit in to be loved, we had better follow suit and act properly. The thoughts that arise from this childhood conclusion make us petrified – one mistake and we're out, is what they have told us for so long that we are not even sure who we are any more. As children and later as adults, we often look as neat as a pin. Our houses are tidy, the admin is done, the work is finished well before the deadline. While others are under the impression that our lives are like a long string of Sundays with everything meticulously working like clockwork, we feel hollow. The journey for us is to thaw the frozen well-mannered shell so our authenticity can come to life again.

The origin of this childhood conclusion

As we grow up, we are all moulded in the codes of what is appropriate in our family, our village, town, city or region, our country or religion. Slowly but surely, we are instructed to observe the written and unwritten rules of how to behave as a member of our particular community. Folk like us dress this way and not that, we talk like this and not like that, we eat these foods and not those, is what our parents model to us. As children their norms are ours, until suddenly we cross a line we didn't know was there. The confusion that arises in this territory is the birthing ground of the fifth and last childhood conclusion.

Here's a classic story: the girl feels uneasy as her family is gossiping about her favourite uncle. Everyone seems to be having a good time talking him down. She doesn't understand why such unkind things are being said. She tries to make the conversation stop, but is overruled, so she goes and sits by herself out of earshot. She wants no part of this slander. When she comes back to the family circle, she doesn't really know how to make the connection again. She feels embarrassed that her family has had a good time at the expense of someone else. When she later brings the incident up with her parents, they wave her objections away: it was all innocent chit-chat, they love her uncle and she shouldn't be so difficult. The girl feels herself stiffen; she cannot marry the malicious muckraking with her parents' casual attitude. The belief that deriding people is wrong feels very precious to her – essential. Yet, the people closest to her seem not to be bothered. Maybe she is the one who just doesn't get it, but then there is this uneasy sense of being embarrassed about her parents that doesn't want to go away.

The girl feels a schism: to not be the odd one out she needs to deny her inner truth – but if she renounces her truth, she pretends to be who she is not. The pressure mounts and the child jumps to a conclusion: in order to fit in she will have to play a role. She will have to feign being like everybody else. She watches how others meet life and begins to copy their comportment. She conforms and adapts, she behaves and denies her own essence.

The childhood conclusion of needing to behave "properly" is also jumped to at a somewhat later age, when the onset of hormones begins to change the body but the child still feels like a child. This may make a boy run out into the schoolyard as fast as he can. He has received good marks and his mother will be proud. He spots her right away, spurts towards her and throws his arms around her middle. "Mom," he says breathlessly while he pushes his head against her tummy, "Mom, I have…" His mother grabs his arms, steps back and, looking around her at the other parents, snaps at him. "Aren't you too old now for these kinds of antics? Come on! You're not a child any more, you know that. Well, what did you want to tell me?"

Hearing the edge in her voice and the charge in her words, the boy realizes he has done something horribly wrong. He wanted to make her proud but he has somehow blown it. Now she is upset. He should apparently not have been so excited in running to her and pressing himself against her. He ought to have restrained himself, walked over at a normal pace, kept an appropriate distance and been composed, like a big boy. He feels a wave of shame at having acted like a child in front of the other parents. He recalls the pleasant sensation of pressing his face against his mother's belly. He is full of love for his mummy, the most beautiful mother of all. She, however, has pushed him away and told him he is too big now to carry on in this manner. The boy concludes he must have crossed an invisible line and caused his mother embarrassment and discomfort. He will be more careful next time. He will curb his impulses and not express his love so spontaneously. He locks his heart and draws his boundaries close. He will not be caught off guard again. If he succeeds in holding his feelings and enthusiasm back, he will always stay within the limits of what is right and proper. So, he stiffens. He freezes. He will keep himself in check from now on.

How to keep up with the pace of children as they grow up? Parents are faced with new situations on a daily basis and might take a wrong turn in a split second. As a child, we don't yet know that life is an awkward and clumsy affair a lot of the time, so we are prone to thinking that embarrassing situations are all our fault.

One minute the young daughter is still a girl, the next she shows all the signs of growing into a woman. She herself might be completely unaware that some expressions of affection begin to border on the sensual or the sexual, and so it may hit her hard when her dad suddenly doesn't want her sitting in his lap any longer out of fear of becoming aroused. She cannot place his sudden stand-offishness. She was just seeking the familiar comfort and closeness. The mother would love to hug her son when she can tell he is troubled, but holds back in the belief that he should no longer feel her breasts. This is why she keeps him at arm's length, while he yearns for the innocent intimacy they used to share.

Children keep a close watch on their parents. Most of us like to gain favour with them and we are prepared to go a long way – in fact, we are willing to sacrifice ourselves if we think this will make them proud. In order to be able to fit in, we metaphorically put our love and authenticity in the fridge and adopt ways of conduct we are sure fits the culture we are part of. From the outside, we look cool, calm and collected, but inside we are well aware we are pretending. Appearing serene we are fooling everyone and that makes us feel shallow, lonely and cold. With this gap between the inner and the outer, we are mortally afraid. Any day now we could be found out as a fraud.

The impostor phenomenon

Underreacting from this fifth childhood conclusion makes us become silent and withdrawn, aware that we could have feelings but feeling frozen, and thinking we are better off without showing messy emotions anyway. Overreacting is when we work harder than anyone else, aiming to be infallible and irreproachable because of the misguided notion that we must not be found out.

The fear of being found out as a poseur was a big issue for me when I first went into therapy. I can still picture the bewildered look on the kind psychologist's face when I tried to convey my fear to her that I was just a front. I attempted to paint my inner picture for her by saying I felt like a Hollywood set, where there is only a facade and the doors open on to nothing but empty space. We soon found ourselves incompatible, but the visits to her at least helped me name the paralyzing fear of being found out as a phoney by people who thought me competent and fun.

I wish I, or my first therapist, had heard of the impostor phenomenon back then. This term was coined by researchers Pauline Clance and Suzanne Imes. In 1978, they published their academic paper on what they defined as "an internal experience of intellectual phoniness". They had conducted their research among women, middle to upper class, mostly white, all of them high achievers. By the time Clance published her book *The Impostor Phenomenon* in 1985, she had discovered that men suffer from this experience just as much as women – they just don't talk about it as easily.

The test Clance developed is still freely available on her website. I am definitely still prone to thoughts generated by the impostor syndrome, I find out as I take the test. Agreeing with statements like "I can give the impression that I am more competent than I really am" and "At times, I feel my success has been due to some kind of luck" gives me a score of 85 points out of 100. Fortunately, I've learned over the years to greet these kinds of thoughts like old friends and go about my day while I leave them to slump on the sofa.

Those of us who score high on Clance's test are in good company. Facebook COO Sheryl Sandberg resurrected interest in this topic when she openly wrote about feeling an impostor in her book *Lean In*. She feels strongly that the conviction that they do not deserve to be where they are is holding women back from stepping up in the business world.

Clance's ongoing research affirms that especially successful people seem to suffer from feeling a mistake must have been made somewhere along the line and the mistake police might be knocking at their door any minute. Joyce Roché was one of the first African-American woman to make a career in business, the first to be named an officer of a Fortune-500 company, former CEO, board director of multinationals and winner of the Women of Power Legacy Award, but she has wrestled with feeling like an impostor for most of her impressive career. From a struggling family in New Orleans, she finally came to the point where she could acknowledge herself as a pioneer as she relates in her personal memoir *The Empress Has No Clothes*. "In a large part," she writes, "the impostor syndrome is fed by the mistaken belief many of us hold that our value is measured by some 'objective' yardstick. We do not recognize our essential worth and are therefore constantly terrified that we will be found lacking. Too many of us fritter away too much time, talent and emotional energy because we are afraid we will not be accepted or acceptable. By its very nature the impostor syndrome isolates us from other people and forces us to keep our innermost feelings secret." She adds another layer as she reflects on having kept her family's poverty hidden, and on not speaking out as one of the few black students in the prestigious universities she attended. "Race is a powerful trigger for impostor feelings. Whether consciously or not, people often make assumptions about others based on the color of their skin. The important thing for each of us to come to terms with is how to be in relation to the assumptions people may make about us."

And the winner is...

What if you're afraid that your success is a fluke, and then you win a prize for all the world to see, and it does actually turn out that a mistake has been made? We probably all remember what happened at the 2017 Oscars. There he was, Damien Chazelle, at 32 the youngest ever to have won Best Director, for his movie *La La Land*. His best friend, composer Justin Hurwitz, had also been granted one for Best Original Score. Emma Stone still stood behind the scenes clutching her statuette for Best Leading Actress in their picture, and then it was time for the big prize. Presenters Faye Dunaway and Warren Beatty looked bemused, or was it old age for the once-glamorous *Bonnie and Clyde* duo, some may have wondered. Beatty started and had Dunaway finish the famous sentence "And the winner is... *La La Land*!" Hugs and kisses, tears and joy in that film's crowd, a little pinching of the lips from the other nominees, and the team behind *La La Land* went up to the stage. Halfway through their happy acceptance speeches, the unthinkable happened live on television, covered by media worldwide and tweeted about instantly. A mistake had been made. The wrong card had been read. The winner was *Moonlight*. Gasps from the spectacularly dressed celebrity congregation as this was announced. "Warren, what did you do?" someone shouted. Beatty explained that when he opened the envelope it said "Emma Stone, *La La Land*". He had been given the wrong card. That's why he took such a long look at Faye, and at the audience. "I wasn't trying to be funny," he said. "It is *Moonlight*, the Best Picture."

This is a nightmare come true: officials broadcasting that a mistake has been made and we need to hand in our prize, shuffle off the stage and go back to our seats glazed and dejected. It was also a nightmare come true for the officials themselves, the two accountants from PwC who, just to be sure, bring two cases with two sets of identical cards for each of the awards, as they and their predecessors have done for the past eight decades. A mix-up happened, as mix-ups do. Emma Stone recuperated quickly, saying she loved making history as this must have been the strangest Oscar ceremony in its 89-year history, she loved *Moonlight* and was delighted for them to have won.

Chazelle had talked about his impostor fear in interviews. One of his previous movies, *Whiplash*, premiered to raves at Sundance 2014 and then the Cannes Film Festival, but its success sent him into an anxiety-ridden tailspin. "My mind tends to skitter to extremes," he has said. "I kept thinking that reviews would get worse, other festivals wouldn't respond, and people would be like, 'Oh, it was a Sundance fluke'." Often, when our worst nightmare scenario actually happens, we prove more resilient than we ever believed we could be. We don't die on the spot from embarrassment. At some point in time we may even be able to see the funny side of what first felt like a disaster. I sincerely hope that the accountants' gaffe didn't send Chazelle tailspinning again but has instead helped him discover the inner sense of joy, zest and self-confidence that many people report experiencing once light is shed on the treachery of the impostor phenomenon.

Negative self-talk

We all have our own version of how we will be unmasked as a pretender. The ongoing inner dialogue that results from this childhood conclusion will tend to run along these lines:

NEGATIVE SELF-TALK

Do I look decent?
Will people see that I understand what the code is here?

Can they tell that I can discern between what is "done" and "not done"?

Have I said something crude?

Have I made a wrong move?

If I slip up, I will be found out as someone who doesn't fit the bill.

I have to hold back and adopt the prevailing norm.

I am not sure where the boundary of what is suitable lies.

I have to conform so I don't accidentally cross that line.

I must be polished and polite.

Forever well-mannered.

Perfect, actually.

I am not a feeling person.

I only exist on the outside.

I have to project an image of being capable and competent at all times.

Inside I feel empty and hollow.

I hold on to what seems to be the standard but in fact I am puzzled about who I am.

I don't feel what others seem to feel.

Sometimes I wonder if I exist at all.

I pretend to.

I display desired behaviour.

I am not real.

In the eyes of the world we may seem flawless. We look like we have the perfect house, marriage, children, job, friends, body, clothes, hairdo, manicure, pedicure, you name it. We play the part like star actors who never take a day off to lounge about. "Do I look good?" is part of the chronic self-questioning, which usually only serves to enhance our insecurity. "Am I dressed for the occasion?" we fret before going to a party, even one thrown by good friends. We don't want to embarrass anyone by coming overdressed. "Should I paint my nails, or better not?" was a thought that plagued me when I prepared to give my TEDx Talk. As if the colour of my nails would be the decisive factor in people seeing me as competent. That is the underlying fear of all these worries about our appearance – that in truth we are incompetent. We don't know anything, never have and never will and one day soon this is bound to come out. The seeming solution of conforming has produced a highly unwanted side effect – a constant fastidious vigilance to make sure no one finds out we are just pretending. We are as afraid of falling short as we would be of being discovered as undercover agents who have no business being where we are.

If this childhood conclusion is not very active in you, this may all sound highly exaggerated. Those of us who are frequently in the grip of it, though, will recognize these endless trains of thought about our appearance. We can be so preoccupied with making a good impression that sometimes we cannot for the life of us think of anything to say. Being somewhat distant and aloof already, we don't always find it easy to make contact – and we can also intimidate those who might want to approach us with our air of perfection. Of course, we lose no time in rebuking ourselves about this weak spot either: we tell ourselves we ought to have more social grace and be more flexible.

Intimate relationships

This childhood conclusion of having to hold ourselves back in expressing love flares up in intimate relationships. The boy will not be caught in a spontaneous act of loving as professing his love is tainted with embarrassment, rebuke and rejection. He grows into a man for whom love and sex are distinctly separate. Sex he can have with everyone but in bed with his life partner he is not that amorous. Permanently smooth operator James Bond brushes a grain of sand from his sleeve after having eliminated dozens of enemy troops, makes a wisecrack and looks his polished self again. "Vodka Martini, shaken, not stirred," is his instruction to bartenders in every exotic spot on earth. Author Ian Fleming knew how to make his character's favourite drink mirror the man. The impeccable Bond is charmed by every superb woman who enters his life, but he is shaken, not stirred. 007 can do sex but love continues to be out of the picture. He remains single, never really touched or committed.

The girl grows into a stand-offish woman who is kind and civil but lacking in emotion. She seems never perturbed or out of balance. Her apartment is as scrupulously pleasant as her mood. She acts according to the rules of what is decent, right and proper. Although like most of us she would really like to have a true love relationship, she feels love mostly in general, for the world at large but not for one person in particular. She suspects that she doesn't really live her life. Not genuinely. Not truly. Depression may be the result of this self-denial, especially when the urge to project an image of perfection is so strong that the gap between the outer and the inner realities only widens. I know, believe me; I've been there. When I was in my thirties, my inner yearning for meaning was far removed from my outer yuppie life. I was a calm, cool and collected businesswoman during the week, while in long winter months of depression I often did not get out of bed all weekend. No one knew. I might show up late at a party because I just couldn't make myself get up earlier. Friends would assume I had had another function to attend before. At least, that is what *I* assumed that they assumed. Maybe they didn't even give my lateness any thought at all.

The most intimate relationship, of course, is the one with ourselves. I used to wonder what was wrong with me when my friends were getting married all over the place and I remained single. I was a girl on the town, but I guess my inner gap showed on the outside, too, much more than I imagined. Then I attended a lecture by Robert Stamboliev on the method of *Voice Dialogue* developed by psychologists Hal and Sidra Stone that he introduced in Europe. I volunteered for a demonstration in front of the audience, and he had me switch into a voice that was relaxed and warm. I was shocked, as I usually allowed this more sensitive part of me to come to the fore only in what I used to call "my secret life", in which I read spiritual books that I kept hidden from friends out of fear of being found flaky. I was a star at pretending. I also always knew deep down that there was more to me, as there is to all of us who painstakingly put our authenticity in the fridge.

Core gifts

We draw a childhood conclusion that we need to pretend because as children our essence was not mirrored back to us, and it is exactly the essence of life that we are interested in. Once we no longer believe the thoughts that tell us what we wear is more important than who we are, we can concentrate on what is essential to us – our loved ones, our work, anything. The more we connect to our own essence, the better we can be at letting what is unimportant fall away. We are excellent planners, because we can set priorities; it is easy for us to see what is paramount and what is secondary. We are good leaders as we keep our focus on what truly matters, both in outcome and in the process of collaboration. We have, in short, a keen eye for essence.

However diligently we have tried to hide it, we are often unconventional. Every new generation treads territory where the previous one hasn't gone. Some pioneering is seen as innovation; in other areas, elders may feel that traditional conventions are being trampled, and will speak out about what, in their eyes, is a disgrace. "All truth passes through three stages. First, it is ridiculed. Second, it is violently opposed. Third, it is accepted as being self-evident," philosopher Arthur Schopenhauer famously said. People who stretch or cross boundaries will always have to face antagonism. When our values were ignored or made fun of in our youth, we shrank inwardly while pretending all was well on the outside. Yet, within us lie the seeds of a future that is different from how things are now. The original unconventional, innovative, quirky and even sometimes outlandish spark is still alive within us. When our authentic expressions of love were rebuked, we stiffened and froze, as in our young minds we took this very personally. In truth, sexual mores change with the times and every generation explores boundaries that seemed fixed to the ones before.

Authenticity is the prize of prizes and our authenticity is not compromised by our adaptive behaviour. Under the guise of perfection, we are utterly and purely who we are. It is my experience that once we dare live on our own terms, our former stern and serious attitude gives way to joy and flexibility, and even some outrageousness as we don't mind any more if we are thought weird or eccentric. In fact, we come to cherish our own quirkiness. As Brené Brown points out, "Authenticity is a collection of choices that we have to make every day. It's about the choice to show up and be real. The choice to be honest. The choice to let our true selves be seen."

Talents honed

"When in Rome do as the Romans do" is what we have taught ourselves from the moment we decided adapting was the way to go. As a result, wherever we find ourselves, within minutes we will understand the local conventions. We know exactly how to dress for trekking through the desert on camelback, going for a job interview or meeting the Queen. Like chameleons we take on the colour of the environment and blend in. When we are aware of this quality, we can employ it constructively. No longer will we feel like we are putting on a show. Now we can truly be the host who makes everyone at a meeting or a party feel at home.

Another quality people will name when describing us is discipline, as it looks exceptionally easy for us to stick to a healthy diet or do regular exercise to keep our body firm and trim. The inner experience, however, is not one of discipline but rather one of priorities and dedication to higher principles that make life worth living. We keep our eye on the goal we want to achieve, and then we do what is needed. No big deal for us – and fortunately, even when we defrost we will keep that useful faculty available to us.

Yet another one is precision. Afraid to make a mistake that would have us excommunicated, we develop a critical eye. We immediately spot a weaving error in yards of material, a typo in a book that has gone unnoticed by seasoned proofreaders or an irregularity in the tiles of a friend's recently redone bathroom floor. It may sound like a curse to notice each and every inconsistency, but as we learn to be more light-hearted we can let little mistakes slip by and use our precision only when it is really needed.

Discretion is a quality we might not value highly enough in ourselves. Not wanting the awful secret of our embarrassing conduct to come to light, nor the embarrassment we felt for our family, we know how to keep secrets. Our highly-developed sense of what to tell whom when is an asset to have in many professions, not just in friendship.

We delivered the behaviours we thought were in order, and order we bring to our life and our work. No wishy-washiness when we're involved: facts will be checked, i's will be dotted and t's will be crossed. We start on a project sooner rather than later, and like to be finished before the deadline so we have ample time to revise once more and make it… as good as can be. No longer striving for perfection, we will still do our utmost to present our best effort.

The authenticity paradox

It is no mortal sin to misread a situation. In fact, it is run of the mill. I recently conducted a playful poll among friends on how much of their work was about solving misunderstandings. Making guesstimates as we shared, the average we came to was more than half of the time.

It is no mortal sin either to show authentic love, even if it is done awkwardly or somewhat inappropriately. Love sometimes is just too big to contain and although we don't want to give offence, it may gush out. Nor, in truth, do any of us need to be ashamed of the circumstances in which we grew up. This, however, is wisdom most of us gain only from hard years of agonizing. The embarrassment we felt or caused as a child has us caught in this paradox:

> **THE PARADOX**
> *If I act authentically, I will be misunderstood or rebuked,*
> *but if I≠ behave according to what is customary, I am not real –*
> *either choice is wrong.*

The thing is, there is no once-and-forever solution to this predicament. Life is messy and awkward, not just when we are trying to find out who we are and how we ought to be as children, but right up to the day we die. What to say and what not to mention remains a question to be pondered, and choices made in the moment may not always be the wisest upon later reflection. This, to be honest, is what makes life interesting; the fact that there is no handbook or official institute that tells us what to do when we don't like a friend's new coat that she is so happily showing off, or when we aren't happy with an intern's best efforts. We have to find a way each and every time. We need to negotiate our responses to be authentic within ourselves, and still have some social grace, but grace that does not diminish our realness.

A healing response

Joyce Roché worked as a domestic, like her mother. In the book and movie *The Help* the movement for black people to gain equal rights is played out between uppity white housewives and their hard-working black domestics who live on the other side of the tracks. When she is fired, the "help" Abileen tells the little girl Mae Mobley to remember everything she has told her. Mae Mobley knows exactly what her dear carer means, and repeats in her slow childish voice, "I is kind, I is smart, I is important."

Self-affirmations that are grounded in the truth get through to our essence. Kindly repeating to ourselves that we are real, that we are exactly as we ought to be, that we are of the essence will help us come out of the stiff shell of appropriateness into the core of our being. Such a mantra will also give the mind something to do as we proceed to give ourselves a healing response. Intuitively we can place our hand on our belly to help ourselves dive under the guise of perfection to get to the actual perfection of our authentic self. We can direct our energy inwards from where we have placed our hand and soon feel the glow of our eternal essence. This glow melts us from the inside out, thaws our rigid boundaries of conformity, warms us to others. We may not know what our authentic self looks like, but we can feel it when it fills us up.

Once we have found the way to our own essence, we can energetically help others when we see that they are tight-lipped and disdainful when people just don't behave the way they should according to their self-imposed strict norms. We can help others thaw and let go of their rigidity by consciously growing the sense of our own authenticity. I never tire of reading Marianne Williamson's wise words that describe this process so beautifully.

"Our deepest fear is not that we are inadequate. Our deepest fear is that we are powerful beyond measure. It is our light, not our darkness that most frightens us. We ask ourselves, 'Who am I to be brilliant, gorgeous, talented, fabulous?' Actually, who are you *not* to be? You are a child of God. Your playing small does not serve the world. There is nothing enlightened about shrinking so that other people won't feel insecure around you. We are all meant to shine, as children do. We were born to manifest the glory of God that is within us. It's not just in some of us; it's in everyone. And as we let our own light shine, we unconsciously give other people permission to do the same. As we are liberated from our own fear, our presence automatically liberates others."

Turning this childhood conclusion

Trying to keep a made-up self-image afloat is not only a highway to burn-out, it is also an existence devoid of meaning when meaning is what we most yearn to live. Turning this childhood conclusion helps us be who we really are.

STEP 1: recognize the thought pattern

We can take note of our painstaking attempts to make a good impression, and clock all thoughts related to that urge. The impostor thoughts, that we will be found out sooner than later, are a second category of thoughts to start to look out for. We can now recognize them as emerging from the time when our inner world was not acknowledged or from our belief that we will conduct ourselves inappropriately if we don't watch out. Every time we think we need to adapt, conform and hold back, we can see the childhood conclusion at work.

STEP 2: shift the focus

Subsequently we can shift the focus to the present moment, to who we have become as a human being of flesh and blood who thoroughly wants to enjoy life and who has warmth and wisdom to share.

STEP 3: thank ourselves

It's been hard work to keep our authenticity and quirkiness hidden from view, which we have for long years. We may now thank that part of us that has done this in order to prevent us from standing alone. From the point of view of a child we concluded that it was best to freeze our true self so the family would remain undisturbed. Sacrificing our authenticity is a deed of love that deserves a big thank-you.

STEP 4: invite the embarrassment from back then

Centred in our self, we can consciously evoke the embarrassment that had us frozen into appropriate conduct. We can allow that panic to resurface, the anxiety that we would surely disconcert others by our unconscious indecency, feel again how it was to have our values trampled. We can tap into that long-standing fear of being found out as a fake. Reliving these fears will not last for more than a few minutes.

STEP 5: be real

Now we have directed the energy to the inner being instead of to the outward appearance, we may defrost further and come to life as the person we truly are. Real people do stupid and silly things, they make mistakes. Life is messy. Better get used to this reality.

The first three steps

Turning the thoughts that arise from this childhood conclusion is a big support in the process of thawing and becoming a warmer, more flexible creature. This brief version can be done any time we notice that we hold back or freeze to avoid being inappropriate. We can still look poised and balanced while inwardly we go through the steps of recognizing and thanking the childhood conclusion and shifting the focus to who we are now.

STEP 1: recognize the thought pattern

This conclusion that we need to conform and fit in has turned us into rather a stand-offish customer. This quality is very useful when it comes to observing our own thoughts. It will make it easy to pay attention to all those times when doubt about whether we are making the right impression plagues us; when the thought that we will finally be found out as a fraud takes hold of us; when we go into pretence. Using our well-honed faculty of observing others, we can now bear witness to the times when we hold back by being polite and diplomatic when we don't need to be. As the ability to spot our adaptive manners grows, the inner signal will start to go off each time we think we have to match what seems to be the norm. This signal will tell us we are at the edge of our comfort zone, which is exactly where we want to stretch it a bit.

STEP 2: shift the focus

We are much more than a good-looking outer shell. All that we have done and accomplished up to now has made us into who we are today. We have surmounted all kinds of obstacles and learned from what we have been through. We have adapted to other people around us on the outside and inside we are still who we always were. Now we concentrate on the human being we have grown to be from the child we once were. By our nature we possess an aptitude for pushing the envelope, so let's thaw from the inside out. Real life is waiting for the real us to step in and fully participate.

STEP 3: thank and celebrate ourselves

This step proposes something out of the ordinary. This childhood conclusion might pipe up with warnings not to move in this preposterous direction, but we are alone with our own thoughts, so who cares? The invitation is to thank the part of our consciousness that has endeavoured to protect us from reproof, indecent behaviour or running the risk of embarrassment. In a time of confusion over our changing body, this part of us has concluded that we had better conform to the prevailing norms and standards. Don't rock the boat, fit in – that was the only choice we felt we could make as young adolescents.

Our fastidious self-control and adaptive powers have contributed to who we have become. Let's thank all those thoughts that admonished us to conform, to fit in, to hold back the expressions of the love we felt and reality as we saw it. Show appreciation to this part of us that thought that we of all people should not make mistakes.

Fully turning this childhood conclusion

Giving up the seemingly utopian existence that earned us the pride of our parents and the approval of society at large is a big ask. A motivation might be the wish to stop obsessing about outer appearances and the impression we make on others. We might be stimulated to relax by an inner sense of emptiness and the notion of missing a certain elasticity. We may feel the time is ripe to take off our inaccessible mask of affability. Maybe friends or a lover might nudge us in this direction. Another good reason to go find our authenticity may be that we want to be able to make love without constraint with the one we give our heart to. We may just want to get real.

Once we step out of Pleasantville, we will gradually melt and evolve into the warm, insightful people we are. This begins with noticing the constrictive thoughts, thanking the part of us that had us conform and putting the focus on who we have become. With genuine interest we can subsequently probe deeper.

STEP 4: invite the embarrassment from back then

The world has ample settings where we can flourish, and people who share our way of thinking and acting. That is a good thing to realize before we invite our old shame or embarrassment to come up. One way to do this is to remember a recent situation in which we were afraid to be different. The other option is to travel back in time to an instance when we decided it would really be better for all concerned if we held back and conformed in our manners.

As we were a little older when drawing this childhood conclusion, we might even have a vivid memory of the painful time that we concluded we were somehow morally reprehensible. We can evoke the dread that we would surely be excommunicated, while staying aware that we have become an adult who can manage if someone did give us the cold shoulder once we showed our true colours. It may take some practice to feel the paralyzing, incapacitating, bone-striking panic of trespassing that marks our manners to this day. If we can allow the fear to offend to rise to the point that we are sure we will be repudiated by everyone we know, we can just sit and endure, weather the inner storm.

Like watching our thoughts, the practice is to have our feelings move through us without falling into the trap of being them, without freezing inwardly and adapting outwardly. We are strong, we can hang on in there, in this horror of mortification. The distress will pass quickly. These feelings seem so strong but once we allow them to move, they will run out of power surprisingly fast.

The terrors of castigation, rejection and being dressed down will dissolve by themselves if we just abide for a minute or two.

STEP 5: live our real life

We have made contact with the anxiety that at any point we could be found out as a fraud, and with the deep-seated fear of being rejected by the ones we love the most. Surviving this agony will soften us from the inside out. The more we do this exercise, the more we will come to life. Over time, in our daily doings we will notice ourselves melting, our bodies becoming less rigid and reactions becoming more flexible. We will be lighter, more vivacious. We will also notice that we feel more confident in voicing an opinion. We have always come across as being quite balanced. Now we can practise bringing our viewpoint not just with poise and equanimity, but also with a light touch and our very own quirky take on things.

It may come as a huge surprise that others are fully aware of our tendency to test frontiers. They have been on to us all along. While we tried so hard to hold back our authenticity, family and friends have long seen through our meticulous mask of perfection, and liked and loved us anyway. They will only rejoice when we let up and allow ourselves space to express who we really are.

A positive present

The line between ethical and unethical is often wafer-thin. There have been professorships in moral philosophy in universities since as early as the 17th century, and the discourse is still going on in today's society. Exchanging views about the problems of a mutual friend – is that being concerned or engaging in gossip? How clean and upright is it to talk with colleagues about a boss who doesn't function well? Is it discreet to mention that we are aware of someone else making an investment in a certain project because we overheard this at a party? Questions such as these have no single straight answer. Most of the time what is right depends upon the intention and the circumstances in which a conversation is being held. Still, it is often hard to draw the line between what is right or respectable and what is not, and yes, sometimes we go wrong. It's live and learn. With our long track record of colouring within the lines, our sensitivity in this area will not leave us, but we need no longer be held in check by it.

The childhood conviction of having to fit in will probably mean we will always remain sensitive to criticism. It takes practice to accept that it is really okay for us, too, to make a wrong call or not have finished a report before the deadline once in a while. It takes some practice to get used to the fact that one wrong remark will not lead to getting us banned forever. At first, we can consciously replace the negative self-talk with thoughts like the ones below. Over time, these will become the kinds of thoughts we have without thinking about it:

POSITIVE SELF-TALK

I am an individual of flesh and blood.
It is delightful for me to feel my love and express it.
I give myself full permission to venture out.
Boundaries are reviewed all the time.
How else would we progress?
I want to be proud of myself.
Not because I appear to lead the perfect life but because of the
    unique person that I am.
I am perfect in my imperfection.
Just like everybody else.
We do our best but we are silly and unpredictable creatures.
That is part of being human.
Learning by doing makes for a rich life experience.
I enjoy spontaneity.
I don't worry about how others perceive me.
I enjoy living without reservation.

I experiment with taking a stance.
Let me be considered a fool from time to time.
I am owning all of me, not just the seemingly sound.
I don't need to judge others for not being up to par.
No one is perfect.
That is reality.
I am real.

No one knows

Making mistakes is still not my strong suit. Even now it happens that when I have sent out an email in which I take a stand, anxiety will course through me. "There we have it" is still one of my first thoughts when a fellow board member wants a word. These frights and thoughts, however, I can now recognize as warning signs that stem from my youth. I have learned to step back and no longer allow myself to think that my professional reputation hangs in the balance every day or that my social life depends on what I wear.

Even more, I have grown fond of the concept that life is one big experiment in which no one really knows what they are doing. Yet we act, we move on, we do our thing as best we can. Each and every day sees unexpected events happen in our own lives as well as in the larger context of the world. We all play our own part and together we create what no one of us could have imagined.

In the end

**The more we are able to step out of the way, the more life can
flow through us unhampered, the more positive our present.**

Turning the negative thoughts that arise from the childhood conclusions
is like making a U-turn. On the highway, when we have missed an exit,
we may have to drive quite a while in the wrong direction before we can turn
back towards our destination. On a country road, we will have to find the
right spot where we can reverse and not present a hazard for other traffic that
cannot see around the bend. I propose that the U-turns we make when we
stop to thank and feel our childhood anxiety, needs, anger, fears and shame be
called you-turns.

You-turns bring us out of the fix. They take us out of the contracted space
of the dependent child where we are fully focused on what we need, back to a
world full of others. Expanding into who we have become brings us back into
relationship, into awareness of what other people may want and need, into
exchanges free of hidden agendas.

Ultimately, life is what happens through us. We can be graceful instru-
ments: welcome, enough, free, courageous and authentic. This is what I have
learned.

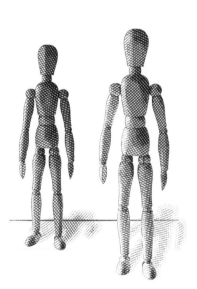

A list of books

I am happy to share a number of books that I found inspiring, thought-provoking and entertaining while researching and writing this book. I've listed them in order of the year of their publication and given short descriptions.

Whose Mind Is It Anyway? (2016)
Lisa and Franco Esile

This charming book of wise words and drawings is good to keep within easy reach. For instance, to be reminded of the Great Grape Trick, which shows the main character with a bunch of grapes on her head, symbolizing her thoughts. Becoming aware that thoughts are not us, but travel through us, lifts the bunch of grapes. And many more adorable reminders of things we know, and keep forgetting.

Getting to Yes with Yourself (2015)
William Ury

Many of us spend over half of our days negotiating, with our spouse, kids, colleagues, bosses and customers. The greatest obstacle to successful agreements and a lasting satisfying relationship is not the other, as difficult as they may be, but our own selves and our natural tendency to react. With his golden tip of "going to the balcony", or taking a little distance from what is happening, Ury shows us how we can make life better for everyone involved.

Dying To Fit In (2015)
Erica McKenzie BSN, RN

She had always believed that what others thought about her was paramount and that changing herself to fit in was the answer to all her troubles. Even while being a happily married nurse and mother, Erica McKenzie was secretly addicted to slimming pills that ultimately sent her to the brink of death. Arguing with God that she wasn't the perfect person to work for him, she discovered that we are all born with unique gifts, and the free will to unlock our power.

The Empress Has No Clothes:
Conquering Self-doubt to Embrace Success (2013)
Joyce Marie Roché

Even having risen to unprecedented heights for an African-American woman in her time, Roché still doubted that she deserved her success and feared being found out. In this heartwarming memoir, former president and CEO of the non-profit Girls Inc, Roché aims to help people, especially in early or mid-career, embrace their accomplishments and success by addressing how she dealt with the impostor phenomenon.

The Whole-Brain Child (2011)
Daniel J. Siegel, M.D., and Tina Payne Bryson, PhD.

Neuroscientist Siegel and parenting expert Payne Bryson offer 12 strategies to foster healthy brain development, revealing their concept of not only a logical left and emotional right brain, but also an instinctive downstairs and a balancing upstairs that is under construction until our mid-20s.

Mindsight – transform your brain
with the new science of kindness (2010)
Daniel J. Siegel, M.D.

Clinical Professor of Psychiatry at UCLA Daniel Siegel proposes a new approach to well-being. Being unable to find an existing term to describe the learnable skill of perceiving our thoughts, feelings, sensations, memories, beliefs, attitudes, dreams, hopes and fantasies, he coined the term mindsight. He shows how conscious cultivation of this skill transforms the physical level of the brain, which in turn helps us direct our thoughts and emotions rather than being run by them.

The Gifts of Imperfection (2010)
Brené Brown, PhD, L.M.S.W.

Authenticity is the daily practice of letting go of who we think we're supposed to be and embracing who we are, according to the definition of writer and research professor Brené Brown. Addressing the audacity of authenticity, in this bestseller she shares ten guideposts on engaging from a place of worthiness, or what she has come to call wholehearted living.

The Biology of Belief (2005–2015)
Bruce Lipton, PhD.

The realization that a cell's life is fundamentally controlled by the physical and energetic environment, with only a small contribution by its genes, set cell biologist Lipton on a trajectory of changing his belief that he was an unsuccessful person to being able to consciously choose his beliefs. The rest is history, as Lipton shows in the additions he wrote to the tenth-anniversary edition of his accessible and ground-breaking book.

Pathways to Bliss (2004)
Joseph Campbell

According to lecturer and writer Joseph Campbell, one of the basic functions of myth is to help us through the journey of life, providing a sort of map to reach fulfilment. His description of the hero's journey is the underlying script of many movies, in which the main character leaves home to face their inner and outer ghosts and comes back wiser and more mature. In this collection of lectures, Campbell examines the personal, psychological side of myth.

Why Love Matters – how affection shapes a baby's brain (2004)
Sue Gerhardt

Love is essential to brain development in the early years of life, so how parents and babies interact has lasting and serious consequences. This psychoanalytic psychotherapist draws on neuroscience, psychology, psychoanalysis and biochemistry to show that the human baby is the most socially influenced creature on earth and that the way they begin to organize their experience affects their later behaviour.

Between Parent and Child (1965–2003)
Dr Haim G. Ginott, revised and updated by Dr Alice Ginott & Dr H. Wallace Goddard

Children cannot help how they feel, but they are responsible for the way they express these feelings. As children learn what they live, the late psychologist Ginott offered empathic communication techniques for parents to model acknowledging rather than arguing and disciplining without threats. The updated version is the work of his wife, a clinical psychologist herself, together with associate professor of family life Goddard. Still a good guide for mindful parents.

A Life's Work: On Becoming a Mother (2001)
Rachel Cusk

This is a disarmingly frank account of motherhood written after the author's first daughter was born and when she was pregnant with the second. Her book met with both delight and criticism; Cusk describes in agonizing detail what it takes to raise a child, and how it drives the parents in different directions. As in her other novels and memoirs, Cusk doesn't just write about strong feelings but also evokes them.

When Things Fall Apart (1997)
Pema Chödrön

American Buddhist nun and poetic author Pema Chödrön shows that moving towards painful situations and becoming intimate with them can open up our hearts in ways we have never before imagined. By being open and non-judgemental we can see and hear and feel who others really are. This book is a gem. Open it at any given page and find an inspiration for the day.

Reclaiming Your Life (1995)
Jean Jenson

Throughout, this book on the benefits of regression therapy gives a felt sense of what it is like to repress and deny feelings after abuse of any kind. Using examples from her private practice, psychotherapist Jenson shows how adults will remain trapped in childhood patterns for as long as they don't process the pain by reliving it, and grieving over it. She also puts forward the insightful notion of overreacting and underreacting.

Light Emerging (1993)
Dr Barbara Ann Brennan

In this sequel to her handbook *Hands of Light*, pioneer of holistic healing Brennan goes deeper into the journey of personal healing and illness, based on her ongoing cutting-edge research into the human aura and the Reichian character defence structures.

Hands of Light (1987)
Dr Barbara Ann Brennan

Three decades in and this is still a classic work on the human energy field. Growing up on a remote farm, Brennan thought it was normal to recognize trees and animals by gauging their fields. After she began to sense people's energy fields, she studied core energetics and several other healing modalities. In 1982, Brennan founded her own healing school, which was granted academic status by the state of Florida.

I Know Why the Caged Bird Sings (1969)
Maya Angelou

In her debut memoir Maya Angelou poetically and powerfully conveys the ache of abandonment when she and her brother Bailey are sent to live with their grandmother, and the agony of having been molested by her mother's boyfriend at age eight. A chilling, gripping, moving account of the struggle that made her into such a formidable woman.

Character Analysis (1933)
Wilhelm Reich

In this learned volume, Austrian psychiatrist, psychoanalyst and sexologist Reich described the underlying patterns he saw in the complaints of his clients. His view is that the age at which we first experience a particular conflict in the child–parent relationship determines the kinds of character traits we tend to develop; that we build our approach to life on only a handful of these conflicts; and that our attempts to avoid painful reactions from our parents contribute to our physical appearance and mannerisms.

A big thank-you

One book is a distillation of the work, thoughts and inspirations of many. Having read this book you will understand that there are many people whom I cannot thank enough.

Dr Barbara Brennan for your persistence, your pioneering work, your healing school, your wonderful team of teachers as well as attracting the colourful bunch of fellow students that made my year into the lively Couch Crowd.

Those who came to my private practice and shared your innermost thoughts and questions with me.

My friends, authors Anneloes Timmerije and Charles den Tex, for nudging me to write as well as for your honest and valuable comments on my first version.

My nieces Nina Schuitemaker and Tessa Kruize for your unwavering faith that this book is of value to your age group.

Robert Coppenhagen, Daniël Doornink and Emma Jansen of Chevigny Publishing for seeing the potential of this book and bringing me to a deeper awareness of what I wanted to say, and Jun-Yi Lee for your hand in the design.

Helen Titchen Beeth and Anna Beeth for your enthusiasm and your first translation.

Anne-Marie Voorhoeve, Marinet Ritz and other colleagues at the Center for Human Emergence, the Netherlands, for integrating my work into our common praxis.

Ingrid Groenen for your lively insight into the childhood conclusion model as you teach it at School of Life, and inspiring conversations over the years.

My heart friend Wies Enthoven for our ongoing conversation on the what and why of life, and all that I learned through co-authoring *The Eldest Daughter Effect* together.

Johan Schaberg for reading through my draft thoroughly, pointing out where I could be clearer and encouraging me along the way.

Sabine Weeke of Findhorn Press for being a staunch and insightful sister throughout the process of rewriting the book to incorporate my grown awareness since its publication in Dutch in 2011. You, too, Thierry Bogliolo, Carol Shaw and Mieke Wik of Findhorn Press, where I am delighted to be, as well as Jacqui Lewis for another fabulous editing job and Damian Keenan for the beautiful design

My partner Jos van Merendonk for your unwavering good humour and for repeating the motto of our relationship "You've got to do what you've got to do" as I sat hidden behind books and cooped up at my laptop, and in my thoughts over dinner.

Most of all, you, my parents, loving Miek and the late Albert Schuitemaker, for giving me exactly the right experiences to set me on my course.

About the author

Lightermaker is how Lisette likes to translate her unpronounceable last name, Schuitemaker, since the old-fashioned Dutch word 'schuit' translates to the equally old-fashioned English word lighter, meaning barge. Apart from being an author, Lisette is Chair of Trustees of the Findhorn Foundation in Scotland, long-time partner of painter Jos van Merendonk, 63-year old eldest daughter of a perky mother, eldest sister to three vivacious siblings, happily childless aunt of eleven, and active inhabitant of Amsterdam, the Netherlands.

With an MA in Classical Latin and Greek from Leiden University Lisette started her own communications agency. After selling this business, she has sat on the board of several forward looking Dutch and European charities. She studied at the renowned Barbara Brennan School of Healing in the United States, obtaining a BSc in Brennan Healing Science. Seeing how much insight Reichian psychology gives, she wrote *The Childhood Conclusions Fix*, which is her third book to be published in English. For more information on Lisette please visit: *lisetteschuitemaker.com*

THE ELDEST DAUGHTER EFFECT
LISETTE SCHUITEMAKER & WIES ENTHOVEN

"What do Angela Merkel, Hillary Rodham Clinton, Christine Lagarde, Oprah Winfrey, Sheryl Sandberg, JK Rowling and Beyoncé have in common?" was the headline in the English newspaper *The Observer* in 2014. "Other than riding high in Forbes list of the world's most powerful women," journalist Tracy McVeigh wrote in answer to her own question, "they are also all firstborn children in their families. Firstborn children really do excel."

Firstborns Lisette Schuitemaker and Wies Enthoven set out to discover the big five qualities that characterize all eldest daughters to some degree. Eldest daughters are responsible, dutiful, thoughtful, expeditious and caring. Being an eldest daughter can have certain advantages, but the overbearing sense of responsibility often gets in the way. *The Eldest Daughter Effect* shows how firstborn girls become who they are and offers insights that can give them more freedom to move. For more info see also *www.eldestdaughtereffect.com*.

978-1-84409-707-4

FINDHORN PRESS

Life-Changing Books

Consult our catalogue online
(with secure order facility) on
www.findhornpress.com

For information on the Findhorn Foundation:
www.findhorn.org